S~~haping~~

a Priestly People

Shaping
a Priestly People

A collection in honour of Archbishop James Hayes
edited by Bernadette Gasslein

Foreword by Raymond J. Lahey
Bishop of St. George's

NOVALIS

Cover and layout: Christiane Lemire

Front cover: Le potier de Jérémie, from *Images de l'Ancien Testament* by Robert Pillods. Used by kind permission of Madame Jacqueline Pillods, Paris, France. Photo: Pierre Lapprand

© 1994, Novalis, Saint Paul University, Ottawa, Ontario, Canada

Business Office: Novalis, P.O. Box 990, Outremont, Quebec
H2V 4S7 Canada

Legal deposit: second trimester 1994,
National Library of Canada and
Bibliothèque Nationale du Québec

ISBN 2-89088-674-3

Printed in Canada

Canadian Cataloguing in Publication Data
Main entry under title:

Shaping a priestly people: a collection in honour of Archbishop James Hayes

1. Catholic Church—Liturgy. 2. Liturgics.
I. Gasslein, Bernadette II. Hayes, James, 1924-

BX1970.S43 1994   264'.02   C94-900429-4

NOVALIS

In grateful recognition

of the ministry of

James Martin Hayes,

Archbishop Emeritus of Halifax,

who has worked tirelessly and lovingly

with many men and women

to shape us into a priestly people.

Pietate concordes

Contents

Foreword

"Your elders shall dream dreams and your young people shall see visions" (Joel 2:28). Every age has its prophets and its pathfinders, those who can speak of what lies beyond the horizon, and those who track a sure way forward. The church of our own day has been blessed abundantly with such prophetic voices and charismatic leaders.

Collectively, the "fathers" of Vatican II—the bishops of the world who assembled in council at the call of John XXIII—were indeed prophets and leaders. Perhaps more than they themselves understood, they gave the church a renewed vision and a clear direction for the future.

Canada's bishops played an important part in the council. In 1962, Bishop Joseph Martin of Nicolet was appointed to the conciliar commission on liturgy. Both he and Gerald Emmett Cardinal Carter, then bishop of London, were elected to the Roman *Consilium* on liturgy in 1964 and 1965 respectively.

When the bishops returned home to their local churches, they were faithful to the council's spirit. Some of these men played a tremendous role in liturgical renewal. Archbishop Michael C. O'Neill of Regina chaired the national liturgical commission. Bishop Carter also chaired the national commission and was a future president of the International Commission on English in the Liturgy. This volume particularly recognizes James Martin Hayes, former

Archbishop of Halifax, twice chairman of the national bishops' commission on liturgy. For him the liturgy and its renewal have been a long-standing labour of love.

These individuals, however, did not toil alone. Only through the dedicated and collaborative efforts of a whole body of people—priests, religious and lay persons as well as bishops—has liturgical renewal made such an impact in Canada. Collectively, these persons were a great blessing to the church in this country. We who are their heirs owe them a tremendous debt. If this volume is dedicated to one man, it is so that through him we might celebrate all those persons—some of whom will never be recognized by name—whose struggle and vision it was to bring together the church's worship and life in the modern world.

We who lived through these years have our own vivid memories of the post-conciliar liturgical renewal. Most often we recall concrete changes— the introduction of the vernacular, the turning around of the altar, the sometimes radical changes in music—for these events tangibly affected the lives of the Catholic people.

Those whose contributions this volume honours, however, understood that the council's vision of liturgy went beyond rubrics or mere pragmatism. Their understanding of liturgy looked past the position of the altar or the style of hymnody to the ultimately profound realities of worshipping our God and sanctifying human existence (*Constitution on the Sacred Liturgy*, 7). These pioneers realized also that the greatest "discovery" of liturgical renewal was not its re-introduction of the vernacular, but its re-focusing on this fundamental principle: From beginning to end the liturgy is the action of Jesus Christ to which his body, the church, is joined "through . . . with . . . and in him." Only this dignity as Christ's members can give sense to the council's most basic proposal for reform—that "all believers. . . be led to take a full, conscious and active part in liturgical celebration"(*CSL* 14). All other changes were important only if and to the degree that they embodied this fundamental principle.

The various contributions of the present volume, different in style and content, reflect this theme. Their common thread seeks to convey not merely *what* happened after Vatican II, but *why* it happened. In their diverse ways these articles underline that inseparable connection between the church itself and the liturgy that is the summit and source of its life (*CSL*, 9). They reflect the fact that liturgical renewal not only changed the church's worship, but the worshipping church itself. To read them is to be renewed in one's conviction of how profound are the realities with which liturgy deals, and how deeply it touches the lives of God's people.

In one sense these chapters are about the past. More than a quarter of a century has passed since Vatican II. To the young, and even to many Catholics approaching middle age, "the council" that stirred so many emotions is now just a vague phrase. This volume's greatest value is its way of recalling this past so that the vision of Vatican II can guide and animate the present. We too must be moved by the realization that the church's celebrations are nothing less than the prayer and work of Christ himself in which we have been given a part. Thus will the vision of our precursors enter into the living tradition that will sustain the church in our own day and shape a priestly people in generations yet to come.

RAYMOND J. LAHEY
Bishop of St. George's

Introduction

Bernadette Gasslein

In my collection of liturgical memories, one scene stands out. Several years ago, I visited the Archdiocese of Halifax for the first time, as one of the speakers at the annual Archdiocesan Youth Festival. The conference opened with evening prayer from the Liturgy of the Hours. Young women and men in their late teens or early twenties carried out all the ministries, including presiding and reflecting on the word. They did this, in the succinct words of Gabe Huck, "with grace and style." And we prayed together, youth and elders, women and men.

Over the years I have heard many stories of the liturgical tradition that Archbishop James Hayes had nurtured in the Archdiocese of Halifax. That evening's prayer embodied the best of that tradition: a sense of the assembled community as God's priestly people, called to praise and to pray for the needs of the world; ministries carried out with care and beauty; a vision of church in which all the baptized are called to minister to the whole body of Christ.

Experiencing this prayer of the church of Halifax on this and subsequent occasions enabled me to understand why James Hayes has had such an impact, not only on the local church, but also on the Canadian church. "We achieve our purpose no better than by joining one another in worship by words, actions and song,"[1] he wrote in 1980. His words are not mere theory; they carry a vision that he has endeavoured to implement locally and nationally since his episcopal ordination in April 1965.

Hayes presented his liturgical vision on the very night of his episcopal ordination, when he spoke to the priests of his diocese:

> Some of our Catholic people (and clergy) still consider liturgy to be rites and ceremonies only. "Getting lay people to sing and read and carry the ciborium won't change the world," they say. This is true if the singing and reading and the offertory procession are merely perfunctory rites. But the council says the divine liturgy, "through which the work of our redemption is accomplished," is the outstanding means whereby the faithful may express in their lives and manifest to others the mystery of Christ and the real nature of the true church.[2]

Hayes is always careful to note that this emphasis on liturgy must not be equated with, or fall into, ritual formalism. He notes in the same address:

> Since what saves are not the sacraments alone, but faith coupled with the sacraments, it is evident that the bishop must perform many other things besides the liturgical function true and proper. He must engage in and promote teaching, guidance and social and apostolic action of all kinds. Otherwise liturgical functions could not produce their full effects in the faithful who would perform them without proper dispositions; they would attend them in a merely external fashion and would not draw from them

the vigorous consequences they are meant to bring about.

Over the years, Hayes has consistently promoted and engaged in this teaching, guidance, and social and apostolic action of all kinds. Stories of his episcopal ministry in the church of Halifax, of which a few have found their way into the pages of this book, embody that reality. So do his words:

> This baptized people of God [the laity] lives and shares the hopes and fears of the five billion members of the human family. His people is called to be a sign and a servant of hope and salvation to all in Jesus Christ.
>
> It would be a travesty to focus our discussions on where to build the fences in our garden when our God loves the whole earth with a love that has no limits.[3]

Hayes has called for this love to be translated into action. His own personal engagements witness to this. After his years in Rome, where he earned his doctorate in canon law, graduating "summa cum laude" in 1957, Hayes returned to Canada, equipped not just to be the chancellor of the diocese, but also to undertake a special ministry to the immigrant Italian community of Halifax. Before going to Rome, Hayes had joined the Sisters of Service in their ministry to immigrants arriving at the port of Halifax. Now, speaking Italian, he was better able to respond to these newcomers and established a chaplaincy to the Italian community.[4]

In the years ahead, he continued to remind the Canadian church of its responsibility to embody this love:

> Homelessness in our richly endowed country is a social evil, a social sin, because the

knowledge, the talent and the resources to correct it exist, if we as Canadians have the political will to act. . . .[5]

Another of Hayes' consistent interests has been the ministry of consolation: pastoral care to the sick and dying. In May 1992, as the keynote speaker at "Through death to life," a national conference on the Order of Christian funerals held at Saint Paul University in Ottawa, he spoke movingly of the role of the Christian community in face of the mysteries of life and death. A year later he wrote in *Celebrate!*:

> The ritual, both in its prayers and its pastoral notes, tells us not only how we can provide spiritual care to the sick, but in remarkable ways, it also shows us how the sick can minister to us who are well. In a truly caring situation, both the patient and the care givers help one another to understand the meaning and to share the burden.[6]

Hayes pushes these caring situations to their limits:

> To me, spending time with the dying person is like the experience of spending time before the blessed sacrament. . . . Sometimes we may talk; most of the time we are just there. But the presence means something.[7]

Hayes' vision is born of experience. Now retired as Archbishop of Halifax, he continues the ministry that so engaged him even when he was in office, active at the local, national and international levels. He is Roman Catholic chaplain at the Halifax Infirmary, a general hospital.

Hayes is also known for his devotion to the work of Christian unity. Instrumental in establishing an inter-church study group of clergy in Halifax, he also encouraged the archdiocese to become a full member of the local council of churches. In 1970, under his leadership, the archdiocese of Halifax cooperated with the Anglican and United Churches of Canada to establish the Atlantic School of Theology (AST). His work in building up the human community was recognized in 1986 when the Canadian Council of Christians and Jews honoured him with a Human Relations Award.

In September 1987, Archbishop Hayes was elected President of the Canadian Conference of Catholic Bishops. He was a member of the National Council of Liturgy from 1968 to 1979. From 1976 to 1979 he served as Canada's representative on the Episcopal Board of the International Commission on English in the Liturgy. He is currently serving his second term as chairperson of the Episcopal Commission for Liturgy of the Canadian Conference of Catholic Bishops. He is a member of Societas Liturgica and the North American Academy of Liturgy.

The enthusiasm with which the various contributors greeted the suggestion of this project testifies to the wide-ranging wisdom and deep insight of James Hayes' impact on liturgy. Even those who do not yet know him personally know his reputation as a leader in this field. Each of the topics of this collection reflects, in its own way, aspects of his abiding and passionate concern for the prayer of God's people.

The motto that Hayes adopted for his episcopacy, *Pietate concordes*, describes that concern. He notes:

> "The Piety" here is liturgical worship, the continuation in the church of Christ's priestly action. By this may we all be *concordes*, made one in love: bishops among themselves in the

Apostolic College, priests in their churches and with their flocks, religious in their communities, lay people in their families and their parishes. In all may there be that concord from our common prayer that brings unity, peace and love in Christ.[8]

He never lost sight of the fundamental importance of this priestly action. Twenty-eight years later he described it in this way:

Every member of the church, the body of Christ, shares the royal, priestly and prophetic role and dignity of Christ, the messiah, God's anointed one. The gospel read at the Chrism Mass presents Jesus at the synagogue of Nazareth declaring Isaiah's prophecy fulfilled: "The Spirit of the Lord is upon me, he has anointed me." In blessing the chrism during this mass, the bishop prays: "Through this sign of chrism grant [those reborn in baptism] royal, priestly and prophetic honour" or "Through anointing [with the Spirit] you give [all who have been reborn in baptism] a share in his royal, priestly and prophetic work." . . . The reference, in the blessing of the oil, to the anointing of Christ as priest of the new covenant and the anointing of all the faithful with the oil, blessed in this way, are ancient sacramental signs and symbols that all the baptized share in the priesthood of Christ. . . .

On this occasion, the entire diocesan church participates in a renewal of its commitment to worship, growth, outreach and caring for its sick and infirm members.

The Chrism Mass. . . is a sacred sign of God's people gathered in the local church, trying to become the Christian community described in

1 Peter: "You are a chosen race, a royal priesthood,
a holy nation, God's own people" (1 Peter 2: 9).[9]

This task of shaping a priestly people belongs, not to any one person, but to the whole community. That we are a priestly people—members of the body of Christ whose very being defines our work as praise and petition on behalf of the world—has been developed in theological reflection. In practice it proves more elusive, perhaps because it demands such consistent, hard work.

It demands, first of all, a profound sense of the dignity of the baptized as the body of Christ, the spirit-filled community of the risen Lord, and an active recognition of this reality when that body performs liturgy. It demands that we speak of and to one another, particularly in the liturgical setting, in words that recognize, reveal and respect this identity. It demands constant care for the shape and performance of the work that most clearly bespeaks and shapes our identity as a priestly people: the liturgy. It insistently invites us to become, in *all* circumstances, who we are when we do this work of the priestly people: icons of the presence of the living Christ.

Some—no, many—wonder if this hard work is worthwhile or productive. My long-standing belief that it is eminently so was confirmed that night in Halifax four years ago. In this celebration of a diocesan church I recognized anew how a priestly people sounds, acts and feels.

For twenty-five years James Martin Hayes led this hard work on behalf of, and in tireless collaboration with, men and women of the local church, and the Canadian church. He has shown us how, and opened a way for all who would follow. It is this work of shaping a priestly people that we salute here.

Notes

1.   Foreword, *Catholic Book of Worship II* (Ottawa: Canadian Conference of Catholic Bishops, 1980).

2.   Address given by Bishop Hayes at Banquet for Priests, Archives of the Canadian Conference of Catholic Bishops. I am grateful to the CCCB for granting me access to these documents.

3.   Address "Open the doors" given by Hayes to the Synod of Bishops, October 1987.

4.   J. Brian Hanington, *Every Popish Person: The Story of Roman Catholicism in Nova Scotia and the Church of Halifax, 1604-1984* (Halifax: The Archdiocese of Halifax, 1984), p. 238.

5.   Christmas message, 1987.

6.   "Pastoral care of the sick," *Celebrate!*, May-June 1993, Volume 32, number 3, pp. 23-26.

7.   "Accompanying the dying," *Celebrate!*, September-October 1993, Volume 32, number 5, p. 23.

8.   Address given by Bishop Hayes at Banquet for Priests, Archives of the Canadian Conference of Catholic Bishops, p. 9.

9.   "The Chrism Mass: a celebration of the whole community," *Celebrate!*, March-April 1993, Volume 32, number 2, p. 21.

Liturgical renewal in Canada immediately after Vatican II

I. The vision
Leonard Sullivan

When the bishops returned from Vatican II in 1965, one of their most urgent duties was to implement the council's vision of Christ, the supreme liturgist, in the midst of his priestly people.

The council had proclaimed a new vision of Christ: the Son of God made truly human, become, by his death and resurrection, the liturgist of his body, the church. What was realized once in history is now celebrated in mystery, through those saving actions by which the church lives and grows. The bishops realized that they fulfil daily Christ's commission to go forth and bring the world into his Spirit-filled body, as they continue, for the good of the whole church, the work of the apostles. All liturgical effort, therefore, requires loving unity: the reform will succeed insofar as it opens itself to embrace all the initiated, gives a place to the charisms of all and does not impede the Spirit.

Christ's action in the church can hardly be seen in a laity reduced to silence, rendered immobile no matter how gifted, never consulted or heeded. Active, responsible ministers working together with the bishop, using the gifts of the Spirit for the good of the community, would be the agents of the reform. The council had done much to educate the bishops. Would the bishops be able to educate the clergy and laity?

The early leaders

After the publication of the *Constitution on the Sacred Liturgy* (December 4, 1963), three bishops led Canadian Catholics into liturgical reform. Each brought a particular vision to this vast enterprise of renewal, the first since the Council of Trent, four hundred years earlier.

• Archbishop Michael O'Neill, of Regina, Saskatchewan, a patrician with a rich background in music and liturgical reading, was co-founder of the International Commission on English in the Liturgy (ICEL). He shepherded the early reforms through the bishops' meetings and attended the first gatherings of the National Council for Liturgy. Through this group, he fostered the idea of a national hymnal, a direct development of his pastoral experience in Saskatchewan, where the dioceses had met for twenty years in music schools led by Monsignors M. Ronan and B. Armstrong from Toronto, and Alexander Peloquin from Boston. The first English-language altar missal in the world (June 1964) bears Archbishop O'Neill's authorization.

• Gerald Emmett Cardinal Carter, then Bishop of London, gave energy and effectiveness to the liturgical reform from 1967 onwards. His appointment by Pope Paul VI to the Congregation of Divine Worship (CDW) on January 5, 1970, gave Canada's liturgists an informed leader who was completely at home with the nation's anglophone and francophone liturgical offices, and with Rome's long-range planners. For several years, he presided over ICEL. On occasion, he chose to bring the Roman liturgical leaders to Canada so that they might experience the vitality of the church here, and see firsthand the need for ecumenical generosity.[1]

• Archbishop James Hayes of Halifax, Nova Scotia, joined the national liturgical leadership following his episcopal ordination in 1965. He brought to the National Council for Liturgy a strongly defined appreciation of what was important in liturgy. His skill as a canonist, as a careful student of liturgical law and documentation, gave us a Canadian version of Washington's Monsignor Frederick McManus. Archbishop Hayes found hidden generosity in decrees and instructions that seemed restrictive and burdensome to others.

James Hayes has the finest liturgical mind among the bishops I have encountered over the past four decades. He has read liturgy for fifty years: his library is filled with books by liturgical and church history masters, giving him access to our ecclesial roots. At times, he offers some arcane bit of liturgical lore, usually to explain how a tradition started. Of particular value is his abiding interest in the development of orders in the Latin rite. Since he knew what a bishop was for, he knew what he should, and should not, do. His efforts in union with the Atlantic bishops to bring the reform to Atlantic Canada have encouraged other sectors of Canada. He has worked as head of the Episcopal Commission in a spirit of understanding, persevering and unfailing kindness.

The International Commission on English in the Liturgy (ICEL)

The English-speaking bishops from many countries, including Canada, realized the importance of a single translation of the liturgical texts and, in 1963, formed ICEL. The Canadian bishops chose Archbishop Michael O'Neill of Regina as the first Canadian representative on ICEL's Episcopal Board. He has been followed by Cardinal Carter, Archbishop Hayes, and Bishops James Mahoney and James Doyle.

The Congregation for Divine Worship (CDW)

One should not discuss Canadian liturgical reform without reference to the CDW in Rome. Pope Paul VI remained, from his election between the first and second sessions of the council (June 21, 1963) until his death fifteen years later, the finest patron and best informed pope the Latin liturgy ever knew. He accomplished his desires through Archbishop Annibale Bugnini, C.M. (1912-1982).

Bugnini began his lifelong liturgical work in 1948, as a Secretary of the Vatican's Commission for General Liturgical Restoration. He took care of the reform before, during and after Vatican II, being at the popes' "liturgical desk" for twenty-seven years. Every significant liturgical document bears his name, every reformed rite issued from his committees.

His removal from CDW in 1975, undeserved and graceless, came too late to allow revisionism to take over. The life work of Paul VI and Bugnini has enriched a whole generation of the church. None of their reforms has been revised. Such permanence is a great compliment to both men.[2]

The 60s and 70s

The liturgical movement in North America was strong in the mid-1960s. The Liturgical Weeks died, however, because they moved into politico-social activism. After 1968, the Liturgical Conference re-organized as an ecumenical body. It celebrated its fiftieth anniversary in 1992-1993.

Impatience with the slow pace of the implementation of the Johannine reform led to excesses and divisions: "underground" masses mushroomed, and some who could not organize the general intercessions did not hesitate to write eucharistic prayers. Music was dreadful as choirs folded and Latin died. Rubrics, even those that made sense, were rejected, and the strain on a church long used to good order was beginning to tell. One wondered if it would be a new age of the Philistines or, conversely, if the good will of thousands of hopeful Catholics would be channelled into new and active participation.

On the positive side, the National Liturgical Office in Ottawa began to function full time as the 1960s ended. The *National Bulletin on Liturgy*, edited from 1972 to 1987 by Monsignor Pat Byrne, appeared in 1965; through it, the bishops gave direction to the reform.

Several critical decisions were made early in the 1970s. The country would have a national hymnal, no matter how meagre the choices for a repertoire, no matter how frustrating the missalette industry in deflecting genuine participation. Fr. John O'Donnell of the London diocese gallantly oversaw *Catholic Books of Worship I* and *II*. Both answered basic needs: decent music declaring the faith and supporting the liturgical action, music useful from coast to coast.

The decision to begin publishing all our liturgical texts in Canada and to refuse entry to U.S.

materials gave the Canadian church freedom, flexibility and identity. Canada's lobbying at ICEL produced sensible changes in its procedures, changes that we advanced based on our national experience. The Grail psalter became international; ICEL's sacramentary appeared with music; ICEL published "camera ready" rituals. A graphic artist was now part of the publishing process. Our liturgical books began to look worthy and attractive, a far cry from the sorry days of loose-leaf, temporary texts.

In the 1960s and 1970s Canadians began formal liturgical studies, usually at the M.A. level. Most chose Notre Dame, Indiana, but several went to San Anselmo, Rome; Catholic University, Washington; St. John's, Collegeville. Saint Paul University, Ottawa, and Newman Theological College, Edmonton, began including liturgical studies in their summer programs. Liturgical expertise was beginning to settle in all across the land.

To complete the Canadian liturgical scene in the years immediately after the council, one must acknowledge the splendid work of the Montreal-based *Office National de Liturgie*. Its most celebrated director, Fr. Gaston Fontaine, CRIC, was architect-in-chief of the new *Lectionary for Mass*, considered by many to be the cornerstone of the entire liturgical reform. While Quebec enjoyed the skills of many graduate liturgists in the period 1968-75, it lacked a publishing arm (almost all texts were done in France), and it never succeeded in breaking free from the missalette industry long enough to produce a hymnal. Nonetheless, the heroic efforts of the Animation liturgique par l'expression et la communication (ALPEC) enriched French Canada's worship.

II. The vision implemented in publication and cooperation
Patrick Byrne

To implement Vatican II's vision of liturgical renewal, the Canadian bishops' program concentrated on four main areas: publication of the official liturgical books, preparation of educational and auxiliary materials, cooperation with diocesan and regional liturgical commissions, and cooperation with other national and international bodies.

Official liturgical books

The English sector bishops undertook to publish almost all the renewed liturgical books as Rome prepared them and the International Commission on English in the Liturgy (ICEL) translated them.[3]

During the 1970s the publications service of the Canadian Conference of Catholic Bishops published a steady stream of liturgical resources: sacramentary; lectionaries; ritual books for the Christian initiation of adults, baptism of children, confirmation, marriage, pastoral care of the sick, reconciliation and funerals. These provided the Canadian church with dignified official liturgical books in a user-friendly format. Other useful pastoral material was added in the appendix of many of the books, as their Roman introductions encouraged. During the 1980s, revised editions of some of the major books were issued, containing updated and expanded resources. This process of revision continues in the 1990s.

Educational materials and auxiliary publications

Vatican II declared that the "full and active sharing on the part of the whole people is of paramount concern."[4] To accomplish this aim, good liturgical books alone are not enough. Providing formation for clergy and lay ministers so that they can celebrate well and share the riches of the renewed liturgy is essential. The bishops' commission on liturgy began this formation with *Liturgical Renewal* in 1964, and founded the *National Bulletin on Liturgy* in 1965. These publications, both in English and in French, continue to serve the Canadian church. In 1972, the *Bulletin* moved from publishing only official documents to a stronger role of education and liturgical formation.[5] Primarily pastoral in scope, its articles, based on liturgy, theology and history, and on the official prayers and documents of the church, explore practical ways to enable all to benefit from the richness of the church's liturgy and tradition.

The national *Liturgical Calendar* appeared in English (instead of Latin) in 1970. It evolved from a simple listing of feasts to become *Guidelines for Pastoral Liturgy,* providing practical help for celebrations in each worshipping community. Its extensive pastoral notes indicate any new regulations or developments, and offer a brief but practical summary of the church's approach today to many areas of liturgy. These guidelines, reviewed each year, always remain up-to-date.

A series of liturgical leaflets, ideal for inserting into parish bulletins, was also developed. The CCCB publishes more extensive studies and documents in *Canadian Studies in Liturgy*.

Work on the national Canadian hymnal, *Catholic Book of Worship*, was begun in 1967 under the guidance of the National Council for Liturgy.

CBW I was issued in 1972, *CBW II* in 1980, and *CBW III* in 1994. When compared, the contents of these three hymnals show the steady growth of Canadian composers, along with a greater maturity in style and taste as the renewal in church music continues. The emphasis on singing the psalms has grown stronger with each edition. Since 1980 it has included aids for celebrating morning and evening prayer in parishes and other groups.

Study editions of the Sunday and weekday lectionaries allow lay readers, musicians and homilists to prepare using a facsimile edition, which reproduces each page of the large edition used in celebrations. In 1976, the CCCB published *Sunday Mass Book* "to enable people to prepare the celebration of the Sunday eucharist and bring them to the devout and active participation which is the goal of the liturgical renewal."[6]

For the 1987-1988 Marian year, books of prayers for leaders and people, and the Roman directory on liturgical aspects of devotion to Mary were prepared in English. The publication of *The Divine Liturgy* in Ukrainian, English and French marked the 1988 celebration of the millennium of the conversion of Vladimir to Christianity. *Penance Celebrations* and *A Book of Blessings* enable those in pastoral work to celebrate liturgically many events in the lives of God's people.

Cooperation: diocesan and regional commissions

At the beginning of the 1970s, the National Council for Liturgy and the National Liturgical Office encouraged the formation of regional liturgical conferences in the West, Ontario and the Atlantic provinces; English-speaking areas in Québec were invited to the meetings of the Ontario and Québec conferences.[7]

These conferences meet once a year in their own region, and every three years as a national group with the National Council for Liturgy. Still active today, they have produced a number of useful publications. Canadian liturgical leaders, such as Halifax's Archbishop James Hayes, note that the national meeting every three years helps Canadians recognize the many gifted people God has given us here in Canada.

Every two years, the bishops' commission on liturgy and the National Council for Liturgy meet with the professors of liturgy from seminaries across Canada. Together they examine progress, concerns and ways to improve liturgical studies in our country.

Cooperation: national and international bodies

Since Vatican II, several encouraging developments have taken place.

In the 1970s, many other Christian churches studied the *Constitution on the Sacred Liturgy* as they revised and updated their own liturgies, using ancient liturgical texts and the writings of the fathers of the church. Gradually, the liturgies of these other churches and our own have begun to be more alike. The Holy Spirit, active in the church's work of liturgical renewal,[8] has been guiding us all towards a greater ecumenical convergence.

Several national and international associations were founded to promote better liturgical studies and research. Ecumenical in makeup and spirit, they include academic societies, pastoral organizations and consultations for the development of shared common texts. Among them: the Canadian Liturgical Society, the Consultation on Common Texts, the International Consultation on English

Texts, the Societas Liturgica, the North American Academy of Liturgy and the English Language Liturgical Consultation.

Two important developments in the past decade have continued the work of liturgical convergence of the major Christian churches. The World Council of Churches' document, *Baptism, Eucharist and Ministry*,[9] has led most churches to re-examine their own basic approaches and to dialogue with different positions or approaches in other churches. In English-speaking North America, the Consultation on Common Texts spent some 20 years in preparing the *Common Lectionary* and the *Revised Common Lectionary*.[10] Members of the National Council for Liturgy and the National Liturgical Office have been involved in the work of the CCT for many years, and continue to be active.

Archbishop Hayes, involved in the national and international scene of liturgical renewal for more than a third of this century, commented recently on these years: "In our generation we have been privileged to take an active part in a strong step forward in the worship and life of our church. In liturgy, in social justice, in ecumenical progress and in a growing awareness of our responsibilities as citizens of this world, we are being called to walk and worship with Jesus, our eternal high priest, in new challenges and developments. I pray that we will all continue to be faithful to the task to which the Spirit of Jesus is calling the church in our day."

III. Carrying on:
the second generation
Regis Halloran

Let generation after generation tell the stories of faith. Learn and be rooted in the Way, the customs, the traditions of the elders; celebrate the great Easter passage of life! Reconcile and console the unloved and broken in spirit.

Let the household of faith, the holy gathering of believers, come and drink at the fountain of living water! Be nourished at the holy banquet of life, and soothed with the oil of gladness.

Let all sing alleluias, for Christ has died, Christ is risen, Christ will come again! Thus the paschal mystery continues to be, for each generation, the *culmen* and *fons*, the apex and the source, of the spiritual journey.

A rich harvest

During the second generation, many gathered in villages, towns and cities throughout our noble land to present a fragrant offering of their talents, personalities, opinions to enable the Canadian liturgical family to worship in spirit and truth. They built on the solid foundation laid by the previous generation. Those charged with the responsibility of charting and piloting the direction of the renewal can take courage from the wisdom of the psalmist: "Those who go out weeping, bearing the seed for sowing, shall come home with shouts of joy, carrying their sheaves" (Ps. 126:6).

Skilled leaders

Whom does the psalmist affirm? Between 1980 and 1994, the Episcopal Commission for Liturgy (ECL) has been chaired by Archbishop James M. Hayes, Bishops James Doyle and Raymond Lahey and, once more, Archbishop Hayes. Held in special memory is Cardinal Flahiff's presence on the commission. His great wisdom and generous support guided liturgical animators through mighty waves and peaceful shoals to a safe harbour where praise and thanks are given to the Holy God!

The ECL navigated the waters of liturgical renewal from the Atlantic to the Pacific to the Arctic, together with the other bishops of the Canadian Conference of Catholic Bishops, their pastoral office, the National Liturgical Office and their advisory group, the National Council for Liturgy. The directors of the office during the second generation were Frs. W. Regis Halloran (1980-86), Murray Kroetsch (1986-90) and John Hibbard (1990-94); assistant director, Msgr. Patrick Byrne (1971-88), and secretary, Dorothy Riopelle. Chairs of the National Council were Dr. J. Frank Henderson (Edmonton), Dr. Mary Schaefer (Halifax) and Mr. Paul Tratnyek (Kitchener).

With joyful shouts and hymns, these servants of the liturgy have come home with arms filled with sheaves.

Stories of faith

Who can forget the dedicated efforts undertaken to enshrine the stories of faith in the church's ritual books—the prayer companions for the assembly and all ministries? The second generation of the lectionary, the Order of Christian Funerals, and the Rite of Christian Initiation of Adults are gifts for the assembly at worship. *A Book of Blessings* (1981) has made an immense contribution to the renewal of blessings in the Christian life. Revisions continue on the sacramentary, the rites of marriage and penance, a ritual for lay presiders and a book of major rites.

Rooted in the Way

Ongoing endeavours to learn anew the mysteries of faith, to become rooted in the Way, have been integral to the fabric of liturgical renewal in Canada. The breadth of topics considered at national and regional meetings vividly illustrates this: inculturation and liturgy, the rites of initiation, Sunday celebrations of the word, social justice and liturgy, ecumenism and liturgy, language and liturgy, ministries and the assembly.

The establishment of the annual Summer Institute in Pastoral Liturgy under the auspices of Saint Paul University, Ottawa, and with the support of the bishops' commission, has assisted many to prepare for and lead liturgical celebrations. Established in 1987, this institute is primarily staffed by Canadian experts in pastoral liturgy. The Summer School in Liturgical Studies at Newman Theological College in Edmonton offers many in the west liturgical education close to home. Other initiatives, such as the Summer School for Musicians arranged by the Ontario Liturgical Conference and the biennial Atlantic Liturgical Congress, bring to many people new insights, skills and solidarity for parish and diocesan liturgical life. All these undertakings help us to realize the truth of the axiom of Prosper of Aquitaine: "Legem credendi lex statuit supplicandi." (The law of prayer establishes the law of belief.)

Every two years, the bishops' commission on liturgy and the National Liturgical Office meet with the professors of liturgy from seminaries across Canada. In a paper delivered at the first meeting of this group in 1981, Archbishop Hayes stated: "Seminaries and programs of formation are set up purposely to form and build communities and they must do all in their power to accomplish that. But the ultimate purpose of the entire exercise is to prepare men to be priests who will be leaders of the worshipping community."[11]

Celebrating our faith
The pastoral visit of Pope John Paul II

This event, celebrated September 9-20, 1984, is forever etched in the faith journey of Canadians. In reflecting on the liturgies of the papal visit a noted Canadian liturgist stated: "The liturgical celebrations were models of what might be done every Sunday: they showed the benefits of good preparation, care for architecture, of the value of excellent music of a variety of styles. Laymen and women were fully validated in their roles as leaders, cantors and ministers of communion, . . . the physically and mentally handicapped among us, the actually and chronically ill were truly at the centre of many of our eucharistic celebrations. . . . John Paul II showed that prayer and ritual of the native peoples, especially at Fort Simpson (delayed until September 20, 1987, due to bad weather) and Midland, are good and have a place in the life of the Catholic church."[12]

On May 20, 1983, the CCCB established the National Liturgy Desk for the Papal Visit. Co-directed by M. Jean-Bernard Allard and myself, it had the national responsibility for planning and developing the liturgical celebrations for the papal visit. In keeping with the principles and experience of liturgical renewal undertaken in Canada, the CCCB published ritual books and documents for these liturgies. At the express wish of Monsignor John Magee, Papal Master of Ceremonies, the sacramentary prepared for the papal masses and other liturgical celebrations in Canada provided the model for other countries planning for papal visits.

Twentieth anniversary of the
Constitution on the Sacred Liturgy

In 1984 Pope John Paul II invited the chairs of episcopal commissions for liturgy and the directors of national liturgical offices to the twentieth anniversary celebration of the *Constitution on the Sacred Liturgy*, held October 23-28, 1984, in the Synod Hall at the Vatican. Taking part in this "serene reflection on the restructuring of the Liturgy as the Council understood and intended it; on its present implementation and pastoral experience"[13] were Bishop Doyle and myself. One of the participants described this historic meeting and celebration as "the most important *conventus* (gathering) in the life of the Church."[14]

Reconcile and console

The mystery of reconciliation lies at heart of the liturgy. From this seat of life comes the imperative "Be reconciled," and the commission, "Be ambassadors of reconciliation." These are the very essence of liturgical life. The adaptations for Canada found in the pastoral notes of the rituals highlight this ministry of reconciliation and consolation. For example, the *Order of Christian Funerals* calls the community to be united in the ministry of consolation to the bereaved.

During this generation there has not been a moment's wavering, either of trust in the liturgy of the church or of its leaders' commitment to liturgical renewal. The words of Pope John Paul testify to this:

> Nor could it have been otherwise: indeed it is above all in the Liturgy that the mystery of the Church is proclaimed, experienced, lived out. In the Liturgy the Church understands herself, is nourished at the table of the Word and the Bread of life, recovers each day the energy to pursue the course that leads to the joy and peace of the "Promised Land."[15]

What joy it is to celebrate with and live among "a chosen race, a royal priesthood, a holy nation, a people set apart!"

Notes

1.   I recall an event that typifies the way Bishop Carter worked. He invited Archbishop Annibale Bugnini, the Secretary of the Congregation for Divine Worship, to stop off in London, Ontario, after some of the Congregation's meetings in Mexico and Washington. While Bugnini enjoyed the sunshine in Carter's back yard, Carter phoned the National Office in Ottawa and asked if there was anything Canadian liturgists wanted from Rome. I suggested we move into optional use of the Apostles' Creed, a change that required Roman authorization; after a minute or so, Bishop Carter had the whole matter settled, and the Apostles' Creed made its entry into the mass in Canada. He was not one to waste time.

2.   Annibale Bugnini worked as secretary under a procession of seven cardinal presidents, beginning with Cardinal C. Micara in 1948, and ending with Cardinal J. Knox in 1975. The most helpful was Cardinal G. Lercaro (1964-68); the rest were either passive participants or, as in the case of Cardinals B. Gut and J. Knox, outright hindrances. Somehow, Bugnini survived. He was appointed pro-nuncio in Iran in 1976, and for the next six years endured the tensions of Islamic fundamentalism, the Ayatollah Khomeini and the American hostage problems.
Students of liturgy will find in Bugnini's meticulous memoirs the living and authentic history of renewal: *The Reform of the Liturgy 1948-1975* (Collegeville: Liturgical Press, 1990). The

texts that issued from his life work are available from the same publisher: *Documents on the Liturgy, 1963-79*. This tome follows the outline and planning done by Gaston Fontaine, CRIC, founding director of *l'Office Nationale de Liturgie*, Montreal. Bugnini and Fontaine were lifelong friends.

3. There are a few exceptions. For example, Publications Service and the National Liturgical Office looked at the possibility of publishing the *Liturgy of the Hours,* but realized that the 6,000-page text in four volumes was beyond the resources of the conference, and agreed to accept the edition published by Catholic Publishing Co. of New York. ICEL chose to publish the *Pontifical* in 1978 as a service to the twenty-seven English-speaking bishops' conferences around the world.

4. See the *Constitution on the Sacred Liturgy*, no. 14, in *Decrees of the Ecumenical Councils, Volume II*, ed. Norman P. Tanner, S.J., (London: Sheed and Ward; Washington: Georgetown University Press, 1990), p. 824.

5. It met the needs of many people, both in Canada and in 44 other nations, according to circulation statistics for 1987, Publications Service, Canadian Conference of Catholic Bishops, Ottawa.

6. Archbishop James M. Hayes, Foreword to *Sunday Mass Book* (Ottawa: Canadian Catholic Conference, 1976), p. 9.

7. See the *Constitution on the Sacred Liturgy,* nos. 43-46.

8. *Ibid.,* no. 43.

9. See *Baptism, Eucharist and Ministry* (Geneva: World Council of Churches, 1982). This document is Faith and Order Paper no. 111.

10. See *Common Lectionary* (New York: The Church Hymnal Corporation, 1983), and its successor, *The Revised Common Lectionary*, Consultation on Common Texts (Winfield, BC: Wood Lake Books, 1992).

11. Unpublished paper, "Liturgy in Seminaries," given at the first meeting of seminary liturgy professors, St. Augustine's Seminary, Toronto, Nov. 17-18, 1981.

12. A report, "Reflections on the Papal Visit," prepared by Dr. J. Frank Henderson, September 1984.

13. An address given by Pope John Paul II to the presidents and directors of National Liturgy Commissions, Synod Hall, Vatican City, October 27, 1984.

14. Intervention of Most Rev. Guilford Young, Archbishop of Hobart, Australia, October 23, 1984, *Report on Convegno*, p. 921.

15. Address of John Paul, October 27, 1984.

Canada, Rome and ICEL: international aspects of liturgical renewal immediately after Vatican II

Gerald Emmett Cardinal Carter

The Second Vatican Council, in session from the autumn months of 1962 through 1965, was full of surprises, particularly for those who came from the New World. Generally speaking, we had not been exposed to the ferment and the movement of new ideas that had germinated in the thinking of the bishops of Europe, particularly those of Germany, France, the Netherlands and, to a lesser degree, the other countries of Europe.

Vatican II was a revelation for me because I had been bishop then for only about seven months. I was perhaps more alerted to the impending changes in the liturgy than most because I had had the advantage of being involved in the catechetical scene for some years. In particular, I had been privileged to attend the catechetical–liturgical meetings held in Eichstätt, Bavaria, West Germany, in the late 1950s. Notions such as the "people of God," "the signs of the times," "the participation of the community in the worship of God," the use of the vernacular in the liturgy—all of these were current coin in the debates of Eichstätt. I became very friendly with some of the great thinkers and leaders of the advancing church, particularly Jesuit Fathers Hofinger and Van Caster, the leaders and professors of Lumen Vitae, Belgium, and Archbishop Elchinger of Strasbourg. I must admit that as I listened and studied in Eichstätt, I had no idea that the small blaze I was witnessing was to burn so brightly at Vatican II.

The dramatic opening of the council has been well recorded and published, first and most importantly, in a series of letters in the *New Yorker* magazine, attributed to a well-known Redemptorist *peritus* observer of the council. The first explosion came almost immediately. When we sat down to the opening session, we were presented with a list of proposed members of the pre-conciliar and conciliar commissions on almost all of the subjects that we were planning to debate. This list, drawn up by the Curia, was certainly a sort of "in-house" recommendation. Led by Cardinal Liénart, some of the leading cardinals and bishops, offended by the failure to consult on this choice, raised opposition. They put forward a motion to adjourn the council for a couple of days to allow the bishops to consult among themselves and not take a pre-cooked list for granted. The story—whether true or not I don't know—is that Pope John, looking out his window at mid-morning, was astounded and terrified to see the doors of St. Peter's open up and the bishops come pouring out. He thought we were walking out on the council and immediately inquired as to the cause of this departure from the planned program. He was relieved to learn that it was simply an adjournment, not an ecclesiastical revolution. After the prescribed delay we came back. After meeting in various groups, we had amended totally the proposed list, replacing it with a new one that was, in the opinion of many of us, far superior. Since these commissions guided the council to some degree from then on (although they never dominated the voting of the whole house), I have always regarded this first action as having two important effects. First, it declared that the council would not be bullied; second, it indicated that the people we wanted on these commissions were those who had the most expertise, not simply those with the best connections inside the Vatican.

Towards the end of the council, Paul VI decided to set up a *Consilium* that would be a working unit once the Fathers of the council had retired to their respective dioceses. All of the major countries were to be represented. The Canadian bishops had elected Bishop Albertus Martin of Nicolet, Québec, to the council's liturgical commission, where he had worked faithfully. Bishop Martin continued this work as a member of the *Consilium,* and I was appointed to it at the end of the council.

We are now looking at the time after the promulgation of the *Constitution on the Sacred Liturgy* on December 4, 1963. The *Consilium*'s work was to put flesh on the bones of that constitution. We are all quite familiar with the major issues: the introduction of the vernacular languages, a revision of the missal and the readings, the new eucharistic prayers, the permission for concelebration under ordinary circumstances, the encouragement of participation, above all through the insistence on the music of the mass, and smaller details, such as the positions of the altar and of the blessed sacrament. Certain misapprehensions grew up after the council; this is as good a time as any to note that there was no question of downgrading any of the sacraments or excluding any popular saints. The feasts of some of the saints were dropped because there was no historical proof of their having existed. But popular devotion to them did not depend on whether or not they were in the calendar: St. George and St. Christopher are among the best known of these. A similar misunderstanding reigned about the use of the sacrament of penance. Unfortunately, a certain number of priests who were leading in education undertook to misinform the youth of the nation; as a result, the practice of confession and the sacrament of penance have suffered greatly.

Devotion to Mary has had a happier history, although, once again, some preachers totally misunderstood the debate about the question of whether Mary should have a decree of her own or whether she should be included in the *Dogmatic Constitution on the Church*. This was the most closely controverted issue at the council and the support for including Mary in the dogmatic decree was passed by only a few votes. Those who so voted had no intention of downgrading the Blessed Virgin, but simply felt that, theologically, she belonged with the rest of the church. I, for one, still do.

When it comes to weighing the achievements or the mistakes of the council, I never hesitate to express my opinion. Our biggest error was in not realizing that our priests and our people were not sitting beside us as we went through the extraordinarily enlightening, educational process that was the council. Consequently, we failed to take the time required for much more thorough catechesis of our people at home once the council closed. We thought that all we had to do was to implement the decrees that were then being issued under the aegis of Pope Paul VI, and that everyone would follow, more or less blindly. This, of course, was not what happened and a few very false paths were undertaken. Opposition to the loss of Latin and to some aspects of the participation of the people in the liturgy, the trivial nature of some of the popularized music, the already mentioned mistakes on the sacrament of penance, etc., all of these could have been avoided—at least to some degree—by a more thorough treatment of the insights we had contemplated in the debates.

Implementing the council's recommendations

Historically speaking, this was now the time of the *Consilium*. The Holy Father had set up this commission composed of approximately twenty prelates—about five cardinals and fifteen bishops from various countries and a number of consultors and advisors.[1] Bishop Martin of Nicolet was appointed to it in 1964, and I was named to it in 1965.

It must not be thought that the *Consilium* was of only one opinion. Matters were debated very deeply and sometimes a bit heatedly. Prelates like Cardinal Felice, Cardinal Confalonieri and a few others were on the conservative side. On the more progressive side were people like Cardinal Lercaro of Bologna who became president, Father Gut who succeeded him and, above all, the man who was the spark plug of the whole operation and later paid for it, Father

Annibale Bugnini. He ended up as an archbishop and a nuncio, more or less in exile.[2]

We met quite frequently, and worked out practically all of the decrees of implementation that we now have in hand and in place in the church. Obviously they had to be signed by the pope before they became law. Once most of our decrees had been finished and put into effect, the Holy Father made the organism permanent by changing it into a congregation, the Congregation for Divine Worship. It was formed by the automatic seating of the cardinals of the *Consilium* plus eight bishops elected by their peers. As one of this latter group, I continued to labour in the liturgy for some years to come. Gradually we stopped meeting when the status quo seemed to be pretty well established. Then most of my work was transferred to the English translations as a member for Canada of the International Commission on English in the Liturgy (ICEL).

I must say that the Canadian bishops were my strength during all this period of liturgical involvement. One of the strongest voices was that of Archbishop Hayes, who has always been a man with a great liturgical sense. I well remember how helpful he was to me, and how many insights he had on our problems. I am delighted to see that this is being recognized.

The birth of ICEL

The challenge now shifted to translating the decrees and the new publications into modern languages. Every major language group was asked to form a working committee to cooperate in translating the new texts. The major English-speaking countries that participated were the United States,

Great Britain, Canada, Australia, New Zealand, Philippines, Scotland and Ireland and a few smaller groups. The name ICEL was chosen: International Commission on English in the Liturgy. Its headquarters were established in Washington, D.C.; its secretaries have always been American citizens. Archbishop Michael O'Neill of Regina was one of its co-founders. To my surprise, the Canadian bishops chose me to follow him as the Canadian representative under the chairmanship first, of Archbishop Hallinan of Atlanta and, a little later, of Cardinal Grey, whom I succeeded as president. Cardinal Grey was a tower of strength; his recent death brought sorrow to all of us.

ICEL was a hard-working group with a sub-committee of experts who worked between meetings and presented their findings to the bishop members. Things were not always easy. ICEL had stormy periods, such as the struggle about the use of "you" rather than "thou" and "thee." Struggles continue to this day, although most people have now become accustomed to the new forms.

Since financing was important, we incorporated ourselves and tried to protect our work by copyright. The worst incident occurred when the British hierarchy, or rather its representatives, used some texts without the proper authorization. The secretariat in Washington decided to sue. The trouble was that the group which had infringed the copyright was the Catholic Truth Society. The situation became acute when we discovered that the president of the Catholic Truth Society was none less than the Cardinal Archbishop of Westminster, Cardinal Heenan. We were on the fringe of a split in ICEL.

As president, I took it upon myself to fly to England to see the English representative on ICEL. Bishop Wheeler, a charming man, received me as the true gentleman he was. We spent a day together and came up with some compromises and solutions, including dropping the lawsuit. It was one of my best diplomatic efforts, but I am not sure that it was ever very much appreciated at the secretariat in Washington! The rift, though prevented, reappeared in a modified form when Great Britain published its own version of the breviary that it still uses, contrary to practice in Canada, the United States and most other English-speaking countries.

I doubt that this is the place to undertake a serious critique of ICEL's work. I believe there can be little doubt that some translations were inspired from an ideological point of view and that some of the translations were quite doubtful and designed to promote these ideologies. In several cases Rome had to intervene, and refused to accept some of the translations that were misleading, and even wrong to the point of being erroneous. But to judge ICEL on the basis of some ideological meanderings would be both unfair and wrong. On the whole, ICEL has rendered great service to the church and, in particular, to the English-speaking countries. If fault there be, it should be ascribed to the bishops who didn't bother to read the new texts in time to correct them where they needed correction.

During my presidency of ICEL, Canada spearheaded some important changes.[3] We resolved the difficulties in devising the English formula of confirmation, the words of the consecration in the mass and several other important translations.

The challenge of creating translations that are beautiful, enduring and contemporary was difficult.

At many times in our deliberations we agreed that we needed a person of genius to give us the type of formulation that has presided in much liturgical work such as the King James Bible, the hymns of Wesley or similar liturgical prayer.

Most people failed to realize that ICEL's work was part of the task of implementing the council's decision to increase and encourage the participation of the people in the liturgy. This meant that much of the liturgy would now be a proclamation. When the liturgy was uttered in a low voice and in Latin only by the priests, proclamation was of little concern. The vernacular liturgy in which the people would participate presented a whole new problem because, in proclamation, the *sound* of the language becomes important.

The most vital expression and dramatization of this challenge was the discussion over the change from the pronoun "thou" and the adjectives "thy" and "thine" to the "you" and "your" forms. There can be no doubt that the "thou" form has a certain dignity to it as an address to God, but it is extremely difficult to use in proclamation. The argument over the formula for confirmation presented another type of difficulty. The English bishops were pushing hard for this form: "I sign thee with the sign of the Holy Spirit." They seemed to forget that repeating the word "sign" when one is confirming about one hundred children would become ferociously offensive. We succeeded in adopting the more usable form, "I sign you with the Gift of the Holy Spirit."

On the whole I enjoyed my experiences, both in the fundamental liturgical reform, and in the work of ICEL. I must express my convictions that the council achieved a great deal in the liturgy and that, on the whole, it has been well served by ICEL. I would like to conclude with the hope that the bishops of the world will remain alert both to the beauty possible in the liturgy, and to the ever-present danger of ideology overwhelming theology.

Notes

1. For a more detailed list of members, see Annibale Bugnini's *The Reform of Liturgy 1948-1975* (Collegeville: The Liturgical Press, 1990), pp. 942-52.

2. Readers looking for a more detailed discussion of Bugnini's story can explore his *The Reform of the Liturgy 1948-1975* (Collegeville: The Liturgical Press, 1990).

3. For further discussion of these changes, see Leonard Sullivan's "Liturgical Renewal in Canada immediately after Vatican II," *The vision*, p. 25.

The church
as communion

Barry Glendinning

Church order has been a sensitive issue ever since the Protestant reformation. Many reformers rejected the priestly role of bishops, putting forward a single, common priesthood of all believers. When that happened, shock waves rippled through western Christendom, and they have been reverberating ever since.

Faced with the reformers' challenge to the ministerial priesthood, the Catholic Church emphasized even more strongly than before the unique nature of the priesthood associated with the sacrament of orders. This focus on the ministerial priesthood, necessary at the time, shunted further into the background the equally venerable priesthood of the whole church. In the popular mind, the church came to be identified, in the first instance, as a hierarchical church.

When the Second Vatican Council gave high profile to the church as the people of God, its goal was undoubtedly to establish a broader foundation for our understanding of the church and to redress the imbalance exacerbated by the reformation debate.

Given our historical situation, however, there were bound to be some misgivings. Does this description of the church as the people of God leave sufficient room for the role of the hierarchy? Taken on its own, is this description too democratic, too egalitarian in sympathy and tone? Is it not important to remember that the church is a mystery with its own unique ways of governance and life?[1]

Questions and discussions of this kind often end in stalemate, with each side defending its particular point of view. There is no reason to believe that such debates will ever be resolved as long as one critical element continues to be left out of the discussions. That element is the Sunday eucharist.

The fact is that we cannot talk sensibly about ecclesiology and church order unless we are prepared to talk about the eucharist. The sacraments structure and give visibility to the church. And the full assembly celebrating Sunday eucharist is the very sacrament of the church, constituting and reconstituting it in time and space and revealing it for what it truly is.

If, then, we want to gain insight into the nature of the church, we need first of all to turn our attention to the celebration of the eucharist. In the Sunday eucharist the church is made present, realized and revealed in the midst of the world. Hence, the eucharist is the fundamental locus for ecclesiology, and all theologizing about the church must begin there.

What a careful scrutiny of the Sunday eucharist will reveal is really quite remarkable. It will reveal a church that, in its essence, is nothing less than *koinonia, communio*, communion of life in the triune God. From the depths of this truth will flow all further understanding of the church.

Paschal mystery, paschal meal

One of the most notable contributions of the Second Vatican Council has been the official recovery of the paschal mystery as the central feature of our Christian lives.[2]

The mystery of Jesus' passage through death to resurrected and glorious life and the passage of the world in him is the very core of the good news of salvation. The church's traditional kerygma has always been expressed in words such as: This Jesus who died has risen from the dead. Not only has he risen from the dead; he has ascended into heaven, where he is established forever as Spirit-filled Lord at the right hand of the Father. And he communicates his Spirit to the whole world so that all peoples in every age may come to share his glory.

This great passage is remembered, proclaimed and celebrated at the heart of the church's eucharist: "Father, we celebrate the memory of Christ, your Son. We, your people and your ministers, recall his passion, his resurrection from the dead, and his ascension into glory..."[3]

Now, to *celebrate* the sacred mysteries is to participate in them, to be drawn into them, to share in them. To celebrate the Christian passover meal is to pass, in Christ, through death to newness of life. The eucharist, then, catches up the world in the paschal mystery of Christ.

The liturgy has always proclaimed and achieved this. Yet, for many centuries prior to Vatican II, the central focus of the church's life had suffered a kind of dislocation. The paschal mystery had given way to the sacrifice of Christ, now, however, understood essentially as his suffering and death.

The processional cross is a case in point.[4] The original processional cross was a marvellous sign of the triumph and victory of Christ. There was no corpus on this cross. Rather, it was a cross with jewels in the place of the nails, a cross proclaiming the passage of Jesus through death to resurrection and glorious, Spirit-filled life.

To all who saw it, the jewelled cross announced the eucharist as the passover meal of the new covenant times, as the sacred action by which the world makes passage with Christ through death to the life of glory.

By the middle ages, popular piety began to stop short and to concentrate heavily on the death of Christ. Artists began to paint such gruesome pictures of the crucifixion that, in some instances, bishops saw fit to ban their public exhibition. Eventually, the figure of the dead Christ appeared on the processional cross as well, and the crucifix became a kind of Catholic faith-expression for the centuries that followed. Catholics came to see the plain cross as an impoverished reformed expression, while reformers could never understand why Catholics "put the figure of the dead Christ on the cross." In our church buildings, a huge crucifix came to occupy the eastern wall, replacing the traditional image of the *pantokrator*, the glorious Christ, Lord of the universe, seated on the throne of power.

A dislocation of this kind is always a matter of serious concern. The sacrifice of Christ came to be identified with his saving death rather than with his saving death *and* resurrection. The eucharist came to be seen as the memorial of his death; a sombre character quite naturally pervaded its celebration.

Happily, Vatican II began the official reconstruction of the paschal character of the church's eucharist. Today we recognize that the sacraments of Christian initiation are rites of Christian passage and that the restored catechumenate has no other purpose than to prepare the world for that passage.

The eucharist is seen once again as the passover meal of the New Testament. Like its Old Testament counterpart, though now in the sparkling dimensions of salvation in Christ, it is the victory feast of the lamb, the freedom festival of the church, and the joyous celebration of the world's liberation.

We recognize once again that the consecrated bread and cup of wine embody the presence of Jesus in his saving passage. For the consecrated bread is at once the bread that is broken and the bread of eternal life. And the consecrated cup of wine is at once the bitter cup that must be drunk and the cup of godly blessings, the cup that overflows unto eternal life.

The recovery of the paschal mystery as the central feature of our Christian lives allows the church to step out boldly as the community that proclaims a paschal faith, that celebrates a paschal feast and that lives a paschal life. In effect, the rediscovery of the paschal mystery changes the whole direction of our celebration, our witness and our lives.

The kingdom feast

Once we have recognized the eucharist as the passover meal of New Testament times, another beautiful picture comes into view. The eucharist is the feast of the kingdom of God.[5]

If the Old Testament passover meal draws the children of Abraham and Sarah out of slavery into the freedom of the promised land, then the New Testament passover meal draws the world out of the bondage of sin into the everlasting freedom of the kingdom of God.

Jesus stands at the centre of all history. The good news that he brings is all about the kingdom of God:

the kingdom of God has come. Through his death and resurrection, Jesus introduces the end times, opens out the final age of the world, inaugurates the long-awaited reign of God.

Already the kingdom makes its entrance into this world. Jesus, the victorious Lord of the universe, has sent the Spirit of Pentecost with power to transform the world. Step by step the kingdom moves forward to its fulfilment, when God will be all in all. The sacraments are the powerful signs of the coming of the reign of God. They announce the arrival of the kingdom and make it present in our midst. And the whole liturgy echoes with allusions to the presence of that kingdom and its feast.

The great doors of the church building are the holy doors that open onto the sacred meal that is the kingdom feast. The opening procession embodies the journey of the world into the dimensions of the kingdom. The incense, so reminiscent of the cloud of the desert journey and the great *shekinah*, tells the story of the dramatic presence of the unseen God, who even now leads us home. The jewelled processional cross proclaims the victory of Christ and reminds us that we enter upon the feast through the sacrificial death and resurrection of the Lord.

The book of the gospels and the burning candles dramatize a journey that we accomplish through the light of the gospel, which is God's wondrous call to salvation. And the grand vesture of the bishop or presbyter who presides bespeaks the glorious robes of kingdom life.

Every part of the liturgy reveals the kingdom dimensions of the feast. "Now, with angels and archangels, and the whole company of heaven, we sing the unending hymn of your praise." "This is the

Lamb of God who takes away the sins of the world. Happy are those who are called to his supper."

The festive table, set in the midst of the assembly of the nations, is the central and final sign of the kingdom feast. "The kingdom of heaven may be compared to a king who gave a wedding banquet for his son."[6] When we read the signs with the eyes of faith, it is the table of that wedding banquet that we see. God has indeed set a festive table in our midst, a table of new and everlasting life.

Even the real presence of Christ in the eucharistic food and drink may be understood in this light. For if this sacred meal is truly the feast of the kingdom of God, then the food and drink of its table can no longer be ordinary bread and wine. It can be nothing less than the food and drink of eternal life. It can be nothing other than the body and blood of Christ.

Once we discern the kingdom nature of the feast, we are seized by joy, that precious gift bestowed on those who sit at table with their God. We want to run to the feast. We want to taste and see the goodness of the Lord. This joy is the special ingredient of Catholic spirituality and life, for Catholics discern even now the presence of the kingdom and its feast.

Yet, this has not always been the case. When we have failed to recognize the feast, we have failed to recognize the kingdom that opens out even now in our midst. At such times in our history we have become rather earth-bound on our journey, plodding along to a destination that is remote and utterly hidden from our view. The failure to discern the feast has, at such times, had a profound and debilitating effect on our Christian lives. At such times we have lost something of our joy. But to recognize the feast is to rediscover our spirituality and our life. To recognize the feast is to recover our joy.

The church as communion

Our recognition of the eucharist as the paschal meal and kingdom feast leads us forward to the final point of our investigation. The eucharist, sacrament of the church, is the sacrament of the communion of the world with God.

The setting is clear enough: the table, sign of shared life, set in the midst of the assembly of the nations; the table, traditionally squarish in form, inviting all peoples from the four points of the compass and the ends of the earth; the table, with its blessing and its shared food and drink, drawing the world into communion of life in God. Have we not always called this sharing, this partaking of the body and blood of Christ, "holy communion"?

The table blessing, the great eucharistic prayer, is the prayer of a world in tune with its God. It is the great hymn of the universe to the glory of its God, its cosmic song of praise.

In the prayer of thanksgiving, the universe reverberates once again with the rhythm of ancient times. It echoes with communion of life in God. The world sings and dances and plays before the Lord. For our God is the God of joy and communion and life. Our God is the Lord of the dance. No wonder the liturgy is sung prayer. No wonder the liturgy is called "divine."

As the Orthodox theologian, Alexander Schmemann, has pointed out so well,[7] the human race alone is able to know the wonders of God. The human race alone is able to raise a voice of thanksgiving in the name of all creation. It is our priestly work to do just that: with arms outstretched, to gather the entire universe into a cosmic hymn of praise to the God of creation and salvation. This is our calling. This is our most noble work. This is our everlasting destiny. This is the liturgy of our lives.

The world is utterly incapable of singing this song of praise so long as it remains self-centred and in sin, so long as it tries to make itself a god. The world can pray this prayer only when it dares to face the living God, only when it hears the good news that penetrates the darkness, only when it has been converted to the Lord. Hence the preparation for the rites of Christian initiation.

Baptism and confirmation are rites of access to the eucharist and its festal life. In baptism we are configured to Jesus in the mystery of his dying and rising. And in confirmation we are made one with him in the mystery of his ascension to Spirit-filled glory and lordship at the right hand of God.[8]

Thus prepared, we enter the eucharistic assembly.[9] There we proclaim the great prayer and table blessing which joins us, along with the angels and saints, to the everlasting self-offering of Jesus, the great high priest, at the throne of God.[10]

In this prayer we consecrate ourselves and the entire world to God. In this prayer we exercise our royal priesthood in Christ: "Through his cross and resurrection, he freed us from sin and death, and called us to the glory that has made us a chosen race, a royal priesthood, a holy nation, a people set apart."[11] Transformed by the power of the Holy Spirit into the new and living temple of God, celebrating communion of life in the heavenly Jerusalem, we become the very sanctuary of God.

In this prayer, the great table blessing of the eucharist, we make our public covenantal vows to the Lord, vows that commit our lives and the whole world to the glory of God. And in holy communion, in our sharing at the eucharistic table, we seal those vows in the body and blood of Christ and are fashioned into the New Testament church. Between God and the world, this covenant is nothing other than the gift of shared life forever, freely and graciously bestowed in holy communion.

In the church's liturgy, we see the unique and marvellous role of the bishop (and of the presbyter who stands in the bishop's place, making him present in the assembly). The bishop, configured to Christ, the good shepherd, officially convokes the great assembly. The bishop, the icon of Christ, presides at the holy table. The bishop, exercising his ministerial priesthood, leads the assembly in the hymn of praise that consecrates the world to God. The bishop offers the holy food and drink of new life to us all.

The bishop, standing in the long line of apostolic succession, makes present in his person the whole church, reaching back through the ages even to the time of the apostles, and reaching outward to the sister churches throughout the world. Thus, in each and every authentic eucharist, the whole church is rendered present and offers praise to God.

In the course of time, several factors conspired to cloud the church's eucharistic witness to the paschal meal, the kingdom feast, and the communion of the world in God.

The first of these was the removal of the table from the midst of the assembly and its placement against the back wall of the place of gathering. As time went by, the remoteness of the table and its blessing exacted a heavy toll on the consciousness of the community and its eucharistic life.

The second factor, not entirely unrelated to the first, was the gradual rupture between the eucharist and the assembly. For century upon century, the assembly and its eucharist had been one. Eventually, however, the assembly lost its importance. Attendance at the eucharist was required, but hardly a requirement for its celebration.

The third factor was the distinction that was made between the sacrifice of the mass and the sacrament of holy communion. The theological construct was problematic, since the entire eucharist is the sacrament of the sacrifice of Christ, the saving manifestation of the sacrificial death and resurrection of the Lord, the paschal mystery played out in the world.

But the real problem was that it gave some kind of credibility to the community's growing practice of attending Sunday mass while neglecting to share in holy communion. Communion became more and more a private matter, something to be "received" according to the spiritual condition and needs of each individual in the assembly. By then we had drifted rather far from the rich vision of the one table, the one holy food and drink, and the unity of the world in God.

The distinction between sacrifice and sacrament led as well to contention about the altar and the table, about the "Catholic" altar of sacrifice and the "Protestant" table of communion. We would not have had such troubles if theologians had remembered the last supper, if they had recognized the antiquity of the sacrificial meal, and if they had understood that the church's prayer of consecration is the table blessing of the feast.

Thanks to the liturgical renewal, the eucharist is being restored in its original and classic form. As a result, we see some things more clearly now. The eucharist is the sacrament of the church; and the eucharist is the sacrament of the communion of the world with its God. The church is a communion.

There are many images of the church: the people of God, the bride of Christ, and so on. Any one of these images may need to be balanced by others. But communion is not an image of the church. Communion is, quite simply, what the church *is*. The eucharist tells us so.

For the sake of a priestly people

In the days and years ahead, there are tasks that must be undertaken if the enterprise of liturgical renewal is to become the bedrock of communal life, and if the church is to stand out ever more brightly as the sign of communion of life with God.

We shall need to articulate a pastoral catechesis deeply rooted in the richness of liturgical expression, a catechesis that prepares the world to enter into the wild and wonderful world of the divine liturgy and to experience there the awesome and mighty works of God; a catechesis that draws the world ever deeper into the celebration of the sacred mysteries of salvation.

We shall need to rediscover the truth, so clearly evidenced in the teaching of the fathers of the church: all theological disciplines should turn again and again to the liturgy, the church's living tradition and the locus of its ordinary teaching.

In this regard, it may be opportune to quote at length from the *Constitution on the Sacred Liturgy*, since the work of theological reconstruction has only just begun.

> The subject of liturgy must be regarded in seminaries and religious houses of studies as a compulsory "core" subject; in theology faculties, it is to be regarded as one of the principal areas of

enquiry. It must be taught both theologically and historically, and also with regard to its spiritual, pastoral, and juridical aspects. Moreover, teachers of other branches of studies, especially dogma, scripture, spirituality and pastoral theology, should see that they give due respect to the mystery which is Christ and the history of salvation, against the background of the intrinsic demands of the subject-matter dealt with specifically by each of them. In this way, the connection between these subjects and the liturgy, and the underlying unity of priestly formation, will become self-evidently clear.[12]

Finally, we shall need to press forward in our renewal of the Sunday celebration. For the liturgy is "the high point towards which the activity of the church is directed, and, simultaneously, the source from which all its power flows out."[13]

We have yet to arrive at a common vision that sees the Sunday eucharist, celebrated in full measure, as the necessary focus of parish renewal and life. And we have yet to recognize the truth so eloquently expressed by Metropolitan Paulos Mar Gregorios:

> The church as the 'ebed-Yahweh, as the true deacon of God, will need to learn to enter the cloud of God's presence and experience God's self-transforming glory—in the new temple, the spiritual house of the church. It is only from that temple that true *diakonia* can emerge.[14]

It is indeed the divine liturgy—the great eucharist that constitutes the church, the sacrament of communion of life in the triune God—that truly shapes a priestly people for the Lord.

The pioneers of post-conciliar liturgical renewal in Canada have rendered a great service to the church, for they have laid a firm foundation for that shaping of a priestly people. It will be the task of the present and of future generations to bring this work to fruition. Those who have laboured so well deserve no less. The church in the days ahead will require no less.

Notes

1.   See, for example, Vittoria Messori, *The Ratzinger Report: An Exclusive Interview on the State of the Church* (San Francisco: Ignatius Press, 1985), pp. 45-53.

2.   *Constitution on the Sacred Liturgy,* article 5, in *Decrees of the Ecumenical Councils,* ed. Norman P. Tanner, S.J., (London: Sheed and Ward, and Washington: Georgetown University Press, 1990), p. 821.

3.   Eucharistic Prayer 1.

4.   See, for example, J. G. Davies, ed., *A New Dictionary of Liturgy and Worship* (London: SCM Press, 1986), p. 201.

5.   See *CSL,* article 8.

6.   Matthew 22:2. See also Luke 14:15-24.

7.   Alexander Schmemann, *For the Life of the World* (New York: St. Vladimir's Seminary Press, 1973), p, 15.

8.   See, for example, Edward Schillebeeckx, *Christ the Sacrament of the Encounter with God* (New York: Sheed and Ward, 1963), pp. 159-69.

9.   Catechumens are dismissed before the liturgy of the eucharist, since they are not yet prepared, through baptism and confirmation, to take part in the great prayer that is the consecration of oneself and of the world to God.

10.   See *CSL,* article 7.

11.   Preface for Sundays in Ordinary Time—1.

12.   *CSL,* article 16.

13.   *CSL,* article 10.

14.   Paulos Mar Gregorios, *The Meaning and Nature of Diakonia* (Geneva: WCC Publications, 1988), p. 13.

Liturgy
and the local church

Archbishop Rembert G. Weakland, O.S.B.

To understand the role of liturgy in the local church one has to begin with a multi-layered vision. Without that vision there is no way of understanding so many texts of the liturgical renewal in our day. At times it is necessary to begin with the ideal, even if today it remains unfulfilled and perhaps, to some modern pragmatists, impossible. This ideal offers the members of the local church a goal toward which they can work, one that helps them come ever closer to what Christian faith is all about. This same goal can serve as a good pastoral instrument to help our people understand what happens in every liturgy.

This multi-layered model or vision of liturgy has three essential and integrated stages. Its fourth stage, the reality of this historical moment in which we live, will be dealt with separately. A fifth and final stage connects liturgy with life.

The three essential layers

The paschal mystery: heart of all liturgy

The first stage presents the historical happenings surrounding the death and resurrection of Jesus Christ and the sending of his Holy Spirit. One cannot, it is true, separate these events from all the sayings and happenings in the whole life of Jesus—from birth to death—but the liturgy concentrates on the paschal mystery, namely, the death, resurrection, and sending of the Spirit. The liturgy relives Good Friday, Easter Sunday and Pentecost. Every liturgy, but most especially the eucharist, takes us back to these historical events. The early liturgists of this century did not hesitate to say that the liturgy "re-presented" the events surrounding the paschal mystery. All liturgy is, thus, historically oriented. It is rooted in what truly happened in Jesus Christ and his dying and rising.

If we fail to centre our attention first on these events, we will miss what liturgy is all about, for these events still affect our lives today. They are redemptive acts determinative of our entry into divine life. Every sacrament shares in its own specific way in this paschal mystery. Although the mystery remains the same in each sacrament, we share in that mystery in a different mode in each sacrament. In baptism we are immersed into the paschal mystery with Christ; Paul calls it "putting on Christ." Eucharist nurtures this new baptismal life, as it too brings the historical events of the paschal mystery to us in our day.

That is why we say that Christ is the centre of every liturgy. The patristic writers did not hesitate to say that Christ is also the principal actor in the liturgy, both the one offered and the one offering.

We must remember that Christ has now ascended to the right hand of his Father. But we cannot conceive of that same Christ now in glory without referring to his sacrifice on the cross and his resurrection from the dead.

Only when we recover this first part of the vision will the sacraments again make sense to us. These signs and symbols refer by essence to the historical events in the life of Jesus Christ. They bring these events into our lives, into the life of each local church. When we see the sacraments as a participation in the Lord's dying and rising, we will realize their importance. Then they will come to life in the local church. One of the aims of the liturgical renewal was this necessary revitalization of all sacraments. Today marriage and reconciliation especially need this revitalization. Only if we recover Christ's presence in the paschal mystery as it is lived and celebrated in these sacraments will they again be meaningful.

Christ and the heavenly liturgy

We might smile when we read in the documents that our liturgy on earth is a sharing by anticipation of the heavenly one.[1] Such a lofty vision, so often far-removed from our personal experience, is the second stage of our vision of liturgy. Yet this vision lies at the core of what it means to belong to the communion of saints, a doctrine that is so fully a part of Catholic identity.

The history of the Byzantine rites shows how important this picture or image of our participation in, or union with, the heavenly liturgy was to them. Liturgy is to take us out of the ordinariness of life and help us concentrate on what is yet to come. Sometimes this is referred to as the eschatological aspect of liturgy. In every mass we make that same hope our own as we speak of waiting for the second coming of Christ. We are following the Lord's command to re-enact the eucharist till his return in glory.

The image of the heavenly liturgy vividly portrays Christ as surrounded by all the saints in glory, engaged in a never-ending sacrifice of praise. During our own liturgies we constantly remember the risen Christ and those saints. Our worship is united to the eternal worship of the risen Christ who is present in the eucharist. While we name only Mary and some of the saints at every eucharist, we are united to all of them: they are never absent from our memory. At special moments we say the longer litany of saints, confident in our realization that all the blessed participate in our liturgy, as we, through Christ, join in theirs. That is why we feel free to pray to them. Before those important events, such as ordinations and the rites of special consecrations, it is important for us to situate ourselves in the midst of this larger heavenly liturgy. Then, as we sing the litany of the saints, we are with the saints and they are with us, in Christ.

The Byzantine churches have kept this aspect of liturgy alive and vigorous. The incense, the icons, the "mystery" that surrounds these celebrations are all meant to help participants enter into this larger heavenly liturgy. In the west we have been more earthly in our celebrations, but we should not emphasize such a distinction too much. The beauty of Gregorian chant and the uplifting quality of Gothic architecture remind us that the elements of mystery and the transcendent are never to be absent from liturgy. In fact, it is precisely the lack of these qualities that has made so many people unhappy with the post-Vatican II liturgical reforms.

The bishop presides at the celebrations of the diocesan church

The third image depicts the bishop celebrating the liturgy, especially the eucharist, surrounded by all the clergy and faithful of his diocese. This image resembles an earthly, inverted mirror-image of the heavenly liturgy.

This third stage might surprise many. Of all the stages in the vision this one probably has undergone the most change throughout the centuries. But this image determines the relationship between the paschal mystery of the dying and rising of Jesus Christ celebrated, on one hand, in the heavenly liturgy, and, on the other, in the local church. This, the oldest liturgical image in the history of the church, comes to us from the early patristic period. It might surprise many to know that fragments of this picture are still present in our documents and very much in evidence during the liturgical reforms of the last decades.

Vatican II's *Constitution on the Sacred Liturgy,* quoting St. Cyprian, sees the liturgy as the celebration of the church, the "sacrament of unity," and emphasizes the importance of the bishop's role.[2] The text is of utmost importance for recapturing that tradition:

> The bishop should be thought of as the high priest of his flock; the life of his people in Christ in some way derives from him and depends on him.
>
> Therefore, everyone should regard the liturgical life of the diocese centring on the bishop, above all in the cathedral church, as of the

highest importance. They should be convinced that the church is displayed with special clarity when the holy people of God, all of them, are actively and fully sharing in the same liturgical celebrations—especially when it is the same eucharist—sharing one prayer at one altar, at which the bishop is presiding, surrounded by his presbyterate and his ministers.[3]

This part of the vision, first articulated by St. Ignatius of Antioch, writing about the year 110, has remained important for the history of liturgy ever since.

Note that this image includes several elements: all the people of the local church worshipping together, around one altar, with the bishop presiding. Since the liturgy is a symbolic act, all the elements of the vision coalesce to form a most powerful symbol for portraying that the eucharist is an act that unites the faith community which shares in the one body of Christ.

All the reforms of the rites of Holy Week begin with this image. They presuppose that somehow everyone, including the clergy, would be able to participate in the bishop's liturgy. We can see at once that dioceses in the time of Ignatius were similar to today's parishes. They were constructed on an urban model in which people could all attend one ceremony because they lived close to one another. This image was at one time a reality.

Some people may recall that, before Vatican II reformed the liturgy, the subdeacon of the mass, stationed at the foot of the altar, held the paten covered with a veil during the eucharistic prayer. For centuries this gesture seemed to be—and was—ritually meaningless, since, severed from its original context, it no longer served any function. Like so many of those rubrics, it was, nevertheless, the remnant of a function that at one time had been real. It was a vestige of that second period when the bishop's liturgy was not accessible to all.

Not surprisingly, the ideal of all the faithful being present for the bishop's mass could not last for ever. Before long, because of the growing number of Christians, the bishop had to share his work with presbyters. His diocese, the local church, was divided into what we now call parishes and the priests were seen as extensions of the bishop and his ministry. Rome further emphasized that concept by the custom of the *fermentum*. Acolytes took a portion of a host consecrated at the mass of the pope, the bishop of Rome, to each priest as he celebrated mass in his parish. (Note that a single parish eucharist was presupposed.) This piece of consecrated host was a sign of the presbyter's unity with the pope as bishop of Rome. The presence of the consecrated host emphasized the unity of the whole diocese as one local church. It showed that unity still existed, even though all were not present physically at the bishop's mass. The subdeacon's act of holding the paten at the foot of the altar was a remnant of this gesture of holding a piece of consecrated host brought from the bishop's mass as a sign of unity throughout the whole diocese. That piece of host was dropped into the chalice in the co-mingling rite after the Our Father.[4]

The image of the bishop's liturgy, with all gathered around the one altar, has a deep theological basis. It proclaims symbolically that we are a eucharistic church. Most theologians of the early church held the view, not that the church makes the eucharist, but that the eucharist makes the church. In this way of thinking, the church is built up by the eucharist, which unites the members of the church with Christ and the salvific events of his life, and with the communion of saints in heaven. The eucharist constitutes the church as the body of Christ, being built up under the action of the Holy Spirit. Celebrating eucharist continues the mission of Jesus Christ.

In contrast, in the west we have tended to see the church as juridically constituted. We talk first about the appointment of Peter and the apostles and the powers given them to bind and to loose. Only then do we go on to talk about the eucharist and the other sacraments. Byzantine theologians are more inclined to see the eucharist as constituting the church. They never have lost sight of the image of the bishop surrounded by believers gathered around the one altar and, thus, receiving the one Christ, under the action of his Spirit.

I doubt very much that, as the faithful attend mass in their parishes today, they view the celebration as one that in some way forms church, united around the bishop, the centre of that unity. Most children will say that they do not know why a bishop's mass is special. They do know that when the man with the curious hat comes down the aisle with his cane, the ceremony will be longer! Under normal circumstances they do not see their pastor as an extension of the bishop's ministry: the bishop is too distant from their faith life and experience. Most of the time they do not know where the cathedral is located, and have no special attachment to that church unless it is their parish. Only if this relationship is explained to them early on and embodied by occasional liturgies with the bishop will this traditional vision of the liturgy become real again.

The contemporary scene

The pastor and his flock gathered around the one altar

We must extend the vision to a fourth stage: the pastor and his flock gathered around the one altar, since this is today's reality. We will have to live with this image, unless all dioceses are reduced in size to perfect again the image of bishop and flock around one altar—a reduction that we all know will not happen. This image must be seen, therefore, as an extension of the image that St. Ignatius presented.

The reforms of the triduum presuppose that all the faithful of a parish can fit into one church building. We know that such a vision is not realistic. Only by renting a large athletic facility could a parish of thousands of people come together! Most of the time many masses are celebrated in a given church. Only on Easter and Christmas do we see the large numbers of people who should be there. Although some have found the triduum very significant in their lives, the numbers are still not large enough to make the buildings seem inadequate.

In this practical, fourth stage of the vision, every mass becomes a symbol of the unity that should exist in the whole parish—among the faithful, with the diocese, and with the universal church. For these reasons, the bishop, as well as the pope, is remembered in the diptychs. This image of the pastor surrounded by his faithful around one altar should bring to mind the other stages of the vision: Christ and the saving events of his life and death, Christ and the heavenly sacrifice of praise, Christ and the bishop and the unity of the diocese, Christ and the pastor and the unity of all the faithful in the parish.

Through the action of the Holy Spirit, all these layers are present together.

Consequences of the multi-layered vision

The consequences of this vision of liturgy in the local church are many.

First of all, a sense of unity must prevail in a parish, as in a diocese and in the whole church. That sense was very real to people like St. Augustine. Since there is but one Christ and one Spirit, there must be but one mind and one heart in the parish. Eucharist and all the sacraments should unite, not divide. This unity is neither a psychological phenomenon where all agree on everything nor a unity of purpose like that of a club or society. The unity of the local church is founded on the eucharist and is, thus, a unity in the one body of Christ. In this sense, it is based on an objective reality: the same divine life that flows through all.

This unity brings with it a sense of the value and dignity of each person, loved by God and the object of the saving acts of Jesus Christ. The eucharist has, then, an aspect that goes beyond the doors of the church building. We see this aspect every year during the Holy Thursday liturgy when we concentrate on the story of the last supper told in John's gospel. The washing of feet establishes our duty, flowing from the eucharist, to serve others. Eucharist means reaching out to others in love as Christ reached out to us.

Eucharist also means seeking to break down the causes of disunity. It is impossible to participate fully in the eucharist and still hold anything against your brother and sister. Forgiveness is a part of the act of breaking bread.

Every local church liturgically constituted through the eucharist must reach out to the needy and those who in one way or another are marginalized. Every eucharistic church must be a healing community.

Another consequence of understanding ourselves as a liturgically constituted local church is that full participation in the liturgy is of the utmost importance for all. That participation, first of all, should include common worship. We had been taught that attendance at Sunday mass was obligatory, but not why. At times the reason that may have been given was that it was our human duty to worship God; church authorities had determined that we should fulfil this obligation by attending mass on Sunday. Rather we should say that participating in Sunday eucharist is necessary so that we be truly in union with other believers, with the diocese, with the universal church. Thus we are united with Christ and the Spirit who make this union possible.

In this vision of the local church, the role of the bishop and the presbyters is not primarily to be authorities or decision-makers, but to be instruments bringing to us the saving events of the death and resurrection of Jesus Christ. In doing this they fulfil Christ's desire that salvation be extended to all and for ever. The concept of instrumentality, somewhat lost in our day, thus can be revived. We will have no renewal of the sacrament of reconciliation, for example, without this larger ecclesial context. Breaches of unity demand symbols of reconciliation and healing.

There has always been a certain fluidity in the history of parishes. The need to create new ones and to merge or close older ones happens often in history and marks our present period. In such times of change it is important to remember the more stable and traditional sense of the diocese and the bishop. This sense is as central to the local church's mission as the original parish. Most people's spiritual life and growth take place in their parish. Here, too, are their loyalties. The larger role of the bishop and the diocese—the local church—sustains the church's life through all the changes that time inevitably brings.

The liturgical role of the bishop and the makeup of the local church also touch the bishop's role in the other sacraments.

Unfortunately, the bishop is known as the conferrer of only two sacraments: orders and confirmation. Seldom do we see a bishop baptizing, presiding at the sacrament of marriage, or anointing the sick. Rare, too, is the bishop who hears confessions. True, the bishop has too much to do already, but there would be much advantage if he could assume a broader role in celebrating the sacraments in his diocese. During parish visitations, for example, a communal anointing of the sick would help maintain the bishop's role for all the sacraments. The Order of Christian Initiation of Adults, especially its Rite of Election, helps maintain this role, too.

The local church and liturgical renewal

A eucharistic community must emphasize the unity, founded on the presence of the Spirit, that flows from common worship. The general atmosphere and caring attitudes of the faithful in the diocese should also show a striving for unity. Unity means a certain understanding and concern one for another. A eucharistic community does not permit factions and constant bickering.

This aspect of the local church, namely, the search for unity, peace, and accord, is especially important today. So many local churches seem divided: the people are argumentative and strident in their criticism. Some make an enormous fuss over accidentals, especially in the liturgy, and disrupt the whole atmosphere of the church. Liturgical renewal has suffered much from this lack of charity.

Since Vatican Council II there have been attempts to make the rites clearer and less encumbered with historical accretions and to permit the faithful to exercise their baptismal rights by full participation. These aspects of renewal have not always been well accepted. No one is totally satisfied with all these initiatives and their results. Some initiatives have been more successful than others. Unfortunately some people have used these differences to disrupt the life of the local church. It is difficult to defend such disruption: it does not lead to deep prayer or help the faithful experience God's presence in the liturgy. So often some people's actions have attempted to destroy the unity that is the hallmark of a eucharistic church.

Liturgical renewal first hoped to build community—community that is not small-minded and exclusive. Building community is also important for understanding the whole purpose of liturgy. The individual would be renewed in and through the community, the church. Our personalist spirituality has made this kind of renewal very difficult. The goal, however, remains clear. By renewing the theology of the local church centred around the bishop and the eucharist, the renewal hoped that a greater sense of community would evolve and that active participation would enhance this concept of unity and community.

Not surprisingly, we have not been totally successful in such a renewal. Today's culture so lacks a sense of the common good that the liturgy is totally countercultural. Membership in the Catholic Church involves belonging to a larger and more stable community, one that is linked, too, to the larger universal church. That is why the emphasis on the local church as the whole diocese is important. People must know that divisiveness on the local church level also destroys union on the universal level. So many see themselves as belonging to the pope's church, and consequently, want to bypass the local church. As if the pope's church could be conceived of as separate from the whole college of bishops and the local churches! We have still much work to do to help people see the liturgy and the liturgical renewal as a point of unity in the local church, binding together all the parishes, and the whole local church to the universal. We are still too parochial in our views to appreciate that the theology behind the liturgical renewal presupposes a sense of community, both local and universal.

The final stage: eucharist and the renewal of the world

The liturgical renewal had still another purpose in mind. Those who were the motivating forces behind that renewal hoped it would lead to a deeper involvement of the faithful in bringing Christ to our culture. Those founders saw a close connection between the liturgy of the eucharist, in particular, and the renewal of the world. The faithful, renewed personally and as a community, could take that renewal to the marketplace. Such a renewal cannot happen when all the community's energies are spent fighting others in the community.

One could call this a fifth image or vision. The other four stages—the historical events of salvation history, the heavenly hosts and their praise of God, the bishop and the liturgy of the local church, and the pastors and the parishes as the extension of the bishop—culminate in the movement of the faithful from the church building to bring Christ to the world and the life of the world back to the liturgy. Liturgy is thus connected with life. Through the liturgy the world and the community of faith come together. This encounter realizes the principle of the incarnation: God came among us, and continues to come among us, to bring to the whole world new meaning and hope.

Because the liturgical renewal was so intimately linked to the renewal of the whole world, the people, the church, the surrounding culture, it is no wonder that such a renewal will take till the end of time. We can now hope that the solid foundation for such a renewal has been laid. The local church must be solid in prayer and in unity, of one mind and heart with its bishop. All of this is symbolized and made real by the image of one eucharist, one altar, one Jesus Christ, one Spirit, one church, one God and Father of us all.

It is good to reflect frequently on this larger vision of liturgy, with all its stages, and thus renew the hope that it bears.

Notes

1. See *The Constitution on the Sacred Liturgy*, no. 8, "In the liturgy on earth, we are sharing by anticipation in the heavenly one, celebrated in the holy city, Jerusalem, the goal towards which we strive as pilgrims, where Christ is, seated at God's right hand, he who is the minister of the saints and of the true tabernacle. We are singing the hymn of God's glory with all the troops of the heavenly army." *Decrees of the Ecumenical Councils*, Norman P. Tanner, S.J., ed. (Georgetown: Georgetown University Press, 1990), p. 822.

2. *Ibid.*, no. 26, p. 826.

3. *Ibid.*, no. 41, p. 829.

4. Josef Andreas Jungmann, S.J., *Missarum Sollemnia: Eine genetische Erklärung der römischen Messe* (Vienna: Herder, 1948) vol. II, p. 379.

Towards
a renewed local church

Marilyn J. Sweet

Those who faithfully discharge the office of
a bishop in the Church may fitly be called
the rafters, by which the whole building is
sustained and protected both from the rain
and from the heat of the sun. . . . Moreover,
the rafters are said to be of cypress, which
tree possesses a greater strength and a
sweetness of smell; and that denotes a
bishop as being at once sound in good
works and fragrant with the grace of
teaching.[1]

In 1965, James Hayes, recently ordained bishop,
returned from the final session of the Second Vatican
Council to accept increased responsibility in the
Archdiocese of Halifax. He entered fully into the
prescribed roles of bishop: he prayed, he governed,
he preached, he taught. An examination of his liturgical preaching and his actions as bishop offers clear
evidence that he took seriously the bishop's responsibility to be the overseer, the watchman, the shepherd responsible for those in his care. His tireless

efforts to promote, through a variety of wide-ranging activities, the vision of church he had come to appreciate at the council marked his twenty-five years of service as archbishop of Halifax. Through the years his has been a respected voice in areas of public policy in the city and in the province. His efforts on behalf of ecumenism led to the founding of the Atlantic School of Theology. He has consistently spoken and acted to promote work for peace and justice. While it is not possible in this forum to study all aspects of his work, a survey of some of the themes of his talks and homilies will indicate the magnitude and the depth of his contribution to church renewal.

Hayes certainly took to heart the words of the *Dogmatic Constitution on the Church*:

> Among the principal tasks of bishop the preaching of the gospel is pre-eminent. For the bishops ... are the authentic teachers ... endowed with the authority of Christ, who preach to the people entrusted to them the faith to be believed; ... they illustrate this faith in the light of the holy Spirit, drawing out of the treasury of revelation new things and old; ... they make it bear fruit and they vigilantly ward off errors that are threatening their flock.[2]

An ecclesiology born of Vatican II

Archbishop Hayes brought back from the council a profound appreciation of the church as the people of God, the body of Christ and the temple of the Holy Spirit. The concept of the church as the people of God includes the sense of pilgrimage: a community of people journeying to the kingdom of God. A pilgrim church is in a process of continual change and growth. The council's effect on Hayes' understanding of church and his strong desire to communicate that understanding to all the people of the archdiocese of Halifax was evident in a series of homily guides he prepared in the late sixties for the Sundays of Lent and Easter. The goals outlined for the homilies express his intention to share the hope for this "new springtime" with all the people of the archdiocese. The series aimed

> to bring home to our people the true spirit of renewal, to engender an openness of mind and a rejection of narrow-mindedness towards the teachings of the Second Vatican Council.[3]

The homily series, which extended from the First Sunday of Lent to Pentecost Sunday, focused directly on developing an understanding of the church and highlighted the responsibility of the laity. One homily in particular was designed

> to point out to our people that the renewal of the church, called for by the documents of the council, depends in great part on a laity that fully understands their own *co-responsibility* for the mission of Christ in the church and in the world.[4]

Co-responsibility and consultation

Hayes continued the effort to involve the people of the archdiocese in the ongoing work of the church of Halifax throughout his entire twenty-five years as bishop. He was committed to sharing the responsibility for the proclamation of the gospel and discernment of the direction in which the Spirit was leading the church. He shared this responsibility in a number of innovative ways. In a 1981 Pentecost homily, addressed to a large gathering of the diocesan church, he said:

The call to pastoral action which I, your bishop, make to you, the gathered people of the church, is more an expression of the needs we have discovered than of specific solutions to those needs. . . . The answer to them is really in ourselves, in the way we work together as members of a church and in cooperation with the gifts and strengths of the Holy Spirit. Such a response cannot be written or printed on paper. It must come from a living, active community that is ready to search out and use its gifts and talents so that every demand can be answered, every service provided, every good work undertaken with generosity and faith. [5]

Consultation was a feature of his episcopacy. The years 1978-79, 1980-81 and 1986-87 saw extensive consultation throughout the archdiocese to determine the priorities for the church of Halifax, and to assess the concerns of the people prior to the 1987 Synod on the Laity in Rome. Specific policy and program decisions, which affected the future direction of the archdiocese, resulted from these consultations. At the 1987 synod, Hayes, speaking in the name of the Canadian Conference of Catholic Bishops, proposed that lay persons participate in future synods. He summed up to the synod participants his personal understanding of the value of consultation:

We also know that where real consultation and participation occur the Holy Spirit leads us through a kind of conversion: The Spirit brings together the living strengths of a local church and renews among its members—laity, religious and ordained members—the dynamism and the direction of the mission. . . . Consultation, even if it is not juridically binding, clearly implies a firm and mutual commitment to listen and to respond.[6]

When Hayes retired in 1990, an in-depth consultation on future needs in pastoral leadership in the archdiocese was underway.

After the council, some commissions—the ecumenical commission and the social affairs commission—were established rather quickly to advise on the work of renewal in the archdiocese. The minutes of the liturgical commission date from the mid-sixties. Through the years, changes were made as necessary, combining or retiring commissions and creating new ones. Hayes worked carefully to establish a priests' senate and a diocesan pastoral council capable of working together as his advisors. He developed the particular responsibilities of diocesan staff and consultative bodies. He was careful to ground such bodies in an ecclesiology that spoke of mutuality, collaboration and subsidiarity as fruits of baptismal responsibility.

> The Vatican Council recognized in the people of God a variety of gifts (charisms) of the Holy Spirit. The ground for shared responsibility in making decisions in the church is found in the baptism all its members share and in the diverse gifts given for the building up of the community. . . . If the gifts of the Spirit are given to all in the church, then shared responsibility is not a cheap borrowing from secular culture, it is rather the recovery of an element in the constitution of the church as well. That means that the priestly office, whether of the bishop or of the presbyter, cannot be thought of apart from or in opposition to the people of God with its diversity of gifts, but rather as a part of that community. Offices are for the service of the community, not to replace it.[7]

A member of a religious order who had served in several other dioceses captured the reality of James Martin Hayes as Archbishop of Halifax. "I met the bishop three times the first week I was here. He came to visit me, we were at the same funeral, and I attended a meeting with him. I had never been in a diocese where the bishop was so accessible. He really is part of the life of this place."

Communion with other bishops

Hayes' appreciation of the role of the bishop is grounded in the early church fathers and the documents of the Vatican II. His sense of communion with bishops through the ages is obvious when he speaks of "My brother Ignatius," and quotes freely from the teachings of the fathers of the early church. He speaks of the bishop's role as a hearer, one who shares his life with the people of God. The bishop is responsible for sound teaching, for the governance and right order of the local church, and the building up of the community. The bishop's responsibilities are twofold: to be in the midst of the local church, witnessing, celebrating and leading, and to be in relationship with the bishops of other local churches, witnessing together to the unity and universality of the Catholic Church. He explained the role of leadership in this way:

> The immediate purpose of the ecclesiastical hierarchy does not reside in itself, but in the people of God journeying to the land of promise.[8]

He gave to the people of the diocese a deep appreciation of the communion of local churches and their unity with the Holy Father through his generous service to the International Commission on English in the Liturgy, to the Canadian Conference of Catholic Bishops, both as its president and as chair for several terms of the Episcopal Commission for Liturgy, through his participation in the 1985 and 1987 synods, his hospitality to visiting bishops and the total dedication of the church of Halifax to the experience of the papal visit in 1984.

Eucharist: centre of church life

Archbishop Hayes often refers to paragraph 41 of the *Constitution on the Sacred Liturgy*:

> The bishop should be thought of as the high priest of his flock; the life of his people in Christ in some way derives from and depends on him.
>
> Therefore, everyone should regard the liturgical life of the diocese centring on the bishop, above all in the cathedral church, as of the highest importance. They should be convinced that the church is displayed with special clarity when the holy people of God, all of them, are actively and fully sharing in the same liturgical celebrations—especially when it is the same eucharist—sharing one prayer at one altar, at which the bishop is presiding, surrounded by his presbyterate and his ministers.[9]

A central expression of the reality of the church of Halifax has been the gathering of many people from throughout the diocese with the deacons and priests to celebrate eucharist with the bishop, at the cathedral. Through his preaching and his active presence at diocesan celebrations, and through the emphasis he gave to the Chrism Mass and ordinations, Hayes always drew attention to this "principal manifestation of the Church."[10]

Archbishop Hayes' preaching and teaching emphasized Augustine's insight that the "church makes the eucharist and the eucharist makes the church." In encouraging a group to recognize itself as a community formed by eucharist, he said:

> When we see Christians making eucharist, we should see the church most clearly . . . When we want to find out what the church is really like, we should simply have to look at what goes on in a celebration of the eucharist.

He carried that vision further, pointing to the need for full and active participation on the part of all members of the church:

> The clarification of roles, the assignment of tasks—by ordination or in some other way, the mutual cooperation among members, the sense of interdependence and solidarity this provides, all conspire to form the lines and structures and institutions that we call "church."[11]

Hayes' deep appreciation of the eucharist as the centre of Christian life and the life blood of the church was evident from the beginning of his episcopacy. In 1967 Hayes formulated this reality in an address to a group of Young Catholic Workers:

> Liturgical worship is the realization of the church at the point where she is most herself: the encounter with God in Christ. Christ, who becomes present in several ways when the liturgy is celebrated, not only exercises and extends his saving activity through the priests and other ministers, he also forms and becomes present to the whole assembly, the community. He makes that community still more what it really is, the holy people of God and the body of Christ on earth. The church's liturgical worship is the worship of Christ Himself, in the Son's relationship to the Father, in and through the church alive in his Spirit.[12]

He was still teaching it in 1989—to seminarians, to liturgical ministers, to parish councils. He delighted in pointing out—as a measure of the significant change in understanding the act of participating in the liturgy—the enormous difference between the opening mass of the Second Vatican Council, and the opening mass of the 1985 Synod.

Any consideration of Archbishop Hayes' contribution to the life of the church of Halifax must address his understanding of ministry and service. Hayes has given countless workshops, seminars, retreats and classes on ministry in all its various shapes and forms. He often spoke of ministry in terms of service and "shared powerlessness." His vision of ministry has always been grounded in baptism and the needs of the community.

> God makes a covenant with a people, a church, a community of initiated people. That is the grand and beautiful reality of grace and mission and sign, a people created in covenant worship, to witness and to serve. . . . Ministries come into existence because this church, this people, has need of servants for specific tasks, and with specific talents. The number, type and character of such servants will vary from time to time as the needs of the church may change. But always the great encompassing reality is the Church, brothers and sisters assembled by God to serve his world. [13]

When speaking of ministry, Hayes emphasizes that the gifts of the Spirit, while given to individuals, are given for the good of the community of faith. They must be balanced with consideration of the needs of the community, and the importance of good order.

He links the requirement for order with the apostolic tradition and ordained ministries, and connects ordination to the community by recognizing that the community must confirm God's call to serve.

In restoring the permanent diaconate, Hayes focused on the call to serve, and the possibility of answering that call in a variety of ways. He highlighted the responsibility of all in ministry to serve the needs of the community of faith, and he connected particular responsibilities with a particular service. Communion ministers, for example, share responsibility for the unity of the body of Christ. Thus they are to care about serving communion in the Sunday assembly, *and* about those confined to home or hospital, and those who have stopped coming to mass.

Growing into the fullness of the body of Christ

While Archbishop Hayes steadfastly spoke of the renewed church and acted in ways that were consonant with his teaching, he was very realistic about conditions in the local church. His recognition that the church is always in the process of growing into the fullness of its identity as the body of Christ was an important counterweight to the difficulties many had with church renewal. In addressing the Task Force on Future Pastoral Leadership in 1990, he said:

> Whether we like it or not, we must admit that the image of the church as a hierarchical, monarchical organization institutionalized by the Council of Trent and perpetuated in canon law, is still the strongest and most common image of the church. . . . The church as communion . . . was strongly presented by the [Second Vatican] Council as the basis of the church, but it was not

SHAPING A PRIESTLY PEOPLE

grasped by the majority of the people. It was easier to stay with the familiar hierarchical clerical church, than to adjust one's vision to return to the old[est] reality, "the community of disciples." It has been said that "clericalism, legalism and triumphalism are hard to root out or control. They are the three most disabling diseases of the church."[14]

Becoming the church envisioned in the documents of the Second Vatican Council is a long, slow process. The excitement of the 1960s and 1970s became the quiet, hard persevering work of the 1980s, and has now turned into the tug-of-war of the 1990s. Carrying forward the daily life of the church is the work of renewal, work for disciples nourished in love by the word of God and the eucharist, and led forward in faith and hope by their shepherds. The work of renewal continues in the church of Halifax, under the leadership of Archbishop Austin Burke. Archbishop Hayes, now retired, continues to serve faithfully in full-time ministry to the sick and the dying in a city hospital, still "sound in good works and fragrant with the grace of teaching."

Notes

1.   From Origen's "Commentary on the Song of Songs," III, 3, ACW 26, quoted in Cunningham, A., *The Bishop in the Church* (Wilmington, Delaware: Michael Glazier, Inc., 1985), p. 27.

2.   *Dogmatic Constitution on the Church*, 25.

3.   Homily outline, Introduction to series, *Spirit of Renewal*, First Sunday of Lent, 1966 (?), Archdiocese of Halifax. All the homiletic materials are taken from Hayes' collection, located at the Catholic Pastoral Centre, Archdiocese of Halifax, Halifax, Nova Scotia.

4.   Homily outline, "The Laity," May 1, 1966. Archdiocese of Halifax.

5.   Hayes, "Call to Pastoral Action," Celebration '81, Pentecost Sunday, June 10, 1981. Archdiocese of Halifax.

6.   Hayes, "On Associating All the Baptized with Future Synods," Synod of Bishops on the Laity, Rome, 1987; as found in E. J., Kilmartin, "Culture and the Praying Church," in M. Schaefer, ed., *Canadian Studies in Liturgy*, #5 (Ottawa: Canadian Conference of Catholic Bishops, 1990), pp. 110-11.

7.   Hayes, "Pastoral Councils and Priests' Senates," undated. Archdiocese of Halifax.

8.   Hayes, "The Hierarchy and Major Superiors," undated, 1967?. An address to the Regional Meeting of the Major Superiors for the Atlantic Provinces. Archdiocese of Halifax.

9.   *Constitution on the Sacred Liturgy*, 41.

10. In *Celebrate!* Vol. 32, No. 2 March-April 1993, pp. 21-24, Hayes writes eloquently of the Chrism Mass as a celebration of the whole community.

11. Hayes, "Liturgy Seminar," Sackville, N.S., June 1977. Archdiocese of Halifax.

12. Hayes, Young Catholic Workers Study Day, January 31, 1967. Archdiocese of Halifax.

13. Hayes, "Charismatic Renewal, Ministries," undated. Archdiocese of Halifax.

14. Hayes, "The Church as Communion," *Report on Future Pastoral Leadership in the Archdiocese of Halifax*. August 6, 1992. Archdiocese of Halifax.

Reared to celebrate in deed and truth

Liturgical renewal in the Archdiocese of Halifax

Romaine Bates, S.C.

On September 19, 1991, the church of Halifax gathered at Saint Mary's Basilica for the installation of Austin Émile Burke as the tenth Archbishop of Halifax. A spirit of celebration filled the air as representatives of all parishes in the diocese filled the beloved old church. Everything was set for a fitting liturgical celebration.

The procession moved forward majestically. The entrance song was full and alive. The tone was set. The people always responded wholeheartedly. Every part of the liturgy that night moved with the dignity and ease born of the involvement of people who know the freedom of the children of God because they have been reared to celebrate in deed and in truth. Archbishop Burke was taken into the hearts of all as, in his own inimitable way, he spoke to our diocesan church.

At the reception that followed, participants savoured the same tone of holy joy. William E. Power, Bishop Emeritus of Antigonish, summed up the experience when he remarked that the celebration of which we had just been part could never have been carried off with so much perfection, yet experienced with so much ease and spontaneity, had Archbishop Hayes not led the church so well in the years since Vatican II.

Before I slept that night, I pondered the whole experience, reflecting on how it had come to be. The result of years and years of truth, years and years of building the spirit of community in a diocesan church had come through with such authenticity.

My own delight in those reflections was found in the fact that I had been actively involved in the church of Halifax while this development was taking place. James Martin Hayes, who had assumed responsibilities as bishop of the church of Halifax in 1965, continued to lead it for the next twenty-five years, and thus became a prime influence in my life. It is from this perspective that I write of the effect of the many liturgical celebrations which found their culmination on that night of September 19, 1991. What follows, therefore, is a series of stories collected from my memories of knowing and working with James Hayes, as he carried out his ministry.

The man

The church of Halifax was blessed that James Martin Hayes was ordained bishop in 1965, while Vatican Council II was still in session. Brian Hanington describes the tenor of the times:

> The documents of Vatican II called for a radical transformation of the church from a principally clerical institution dispensing doctrine and sacramental grace, to a body of people called to live such a life of truth, justice, faith and love that they would transform the world.

The documents of the council threw the
church into upheaval. Conservative elements
argued that the proper authority of the church
was being undermined. Liberal elements
maintained that the documents hadn't taken the
church far enough, for the implementation of the
changes was by no means guaranteed. The
tensions that arose were many. The post-conciliar
church was hailed by some as a "New Pentecost"
and by others as a disastrous mistake.[1]

As the documents of Vatican II became known,
Archbishop Hayes faced a lack of unanimity in the
local church about their meaning. Naturally, some
resisted what was being proposed. It would have
been easy to give in or give up. Yet he kept on.

Two months prior to his episcopal ordination,
the *Halifax Chronicle-Herald* had carried this
announcement:

A self-effacing, quiet man, beloved of his
own congregation, highly regarded by
Catholic and Protestant clergy, vitally interested
in people, and the youngest rector ever to be
appointed to St. Mary's Basilica is to be the new
auxiliary bishop to Most Rev. J. G. Berry,
Archbishop of Halifax.[2]

This self-effacing, quiet man allowed himself to
be used by God to such an extent that latent qualities
within him developed and flowered. Although it
was not his natural bent, he took on the public role of
bishop with a zest and a presence that were
irreproachable. Once accused by his clerical peers of
"going to every dog-fight in town" because he was
leaving their social gathering to go to another group,
he asked who, then, would go as his delegate and

speak to the group on the presence of the bishop to his people. What more could they say?

He was a man who, when first ordained, would not have been considered a gifted preacher, yet his ability in this medium grew beyond bounds in the years of his episcopate. By nature an introvert, by grace he grew to seem to be an extrovert. He had always seemed serious by nature, yet showed a deep sense of humour as his preaching came alive. He became more and more at home with holy scripture.

He would never have been considered a man to make small talk, yet he could be at home with the simplest, most ordinary people. One morning, after a bitterly cold night, a homeless man was found dead. The only identification he carried was a scrap of paper in his pocket on which a phone number was written. When the police traced it, they found it was the bishop's. This man was buried with the full rites of the church and with the honour given any dignitary.

Good liturgy does not just happen. It takes years of bonding, sometimes in minuscule but still so valuable ways, as the bit-by-bit melding together finally sets. The human presence of the people involved, the presider and ourselves, is so very important to the way liturgy is loved and lived. James Hayes is someone who established a relationship with those who celebrate with him. Perhaps without even realizing it, we experienced him as someone who prays, who cares for others in their joys and sorrows, who knows what is happening in the hearts of those gathered round him, and who thus knows what should be part of the gift we are all offering together.

Establishment of a juniorate

In the early 1960s the Sisters of Charity established a juniorate community, near Mount Saint Vincent Motherhouse, where the newly-professed sisters continued their formation. When this community began, Father James Hayes was chancellor of the diocese, and unattached to a city parish; I was director of the juniorate. He became our chaplain and wonderful things happened as we lived our liturgy.

One day, these young sisters asked about having a mass with the priest facing the people. When Father Hayes first approached Archbishop Berry, the request was refused. The archbishop was asking *why*: why would we be making this request? Father Hayes advised the sisters to prepare a brief to send to the archbishop, to research it thoroughly and to include anything that might influence a bishop to see this as a good thing for his people. In time the permission was granted and gave us great joy.

The faith of the people led him

In the 1970s I was part of archdiocesan happenings from a different perspective. It was then that, as director of religious education for the archdiocese, I could experience liturgy in many different parishes and notice the effects of a deepening understanding of what had been proposed to us at Vatican II.

Our mode of celebrating the sacraments underwent some change. Here again, the thinking of this "people-person" was evident. No longer would Archbishop Hayes confirm huge numbers of candidates at the same celebration. Consequently, some parishes had as many as three celebrations of confirmation during the same season.

On one occasion, at Saint Pius X parish in Halifax, something memorable happened. Our diocesan custom had been to have the candidates for confirmation seated together, boys on one side, girls on the other. We felt that this allowed for ease of communication when addressing candidates or parents separately. In this particular year, the parents resisted, asking instead that they sit as family groups. The archbishop, sensitive to their wishes, responded positively. A truly wonderful thing happened. When he wished to speak to the parents/guardians, he asked them to stand and to place their hand on the shoulder of their kneeling child. He spoke to them of praying in those moments for their offspring, reminding them that, because they knew their child better than anyone else, they knew what to ask the Lord for. It was a solemn moment in the ceremony as they prayed for their children. Afterwards, when I spoke to Archbishop Hayes about how the celebration had impressed me, he pointed out that he had not planned to do it that way: the faith of the people had drawn him to do as he had done.

Going the extra mile

I recall, too, Archbishop Hayes' willingness to "go the extra mile" because of the people involved. On one occasion I recall a confirmation at Lower Prospect on a very stormy night. Following the ceremony Archbishop Hayes sought out a boy who had been accompanied only by a sibling, and learned that he had known the lad's parents at the time of their marriage. So he drove the children home and stayed to visit with the family, an example of the kind of outreach that shows his continued concern that marriages flourish. He is known, too, for his kindness to those whose situation has led them to the marriage tribunal. Every effort has been made to bring peace to troubled hearts by having work done efficiently, quickly and with loving concern.

Renewal of orders

In our diocese, esteem of and love for the eucharist and celebration of holy orders always have been strong in the hearts of many. The years following Vatican II showed that more people were gaining insights into, and grasping the importance of, the communal bond created and recreated in our hearts as we experience the power of the eucharist.

I recall being at Holy Heart Seminary for ordination rites prior to Vatican II. In those days the congregation was small, composed mainly of immediate family members and close friends. We all knew that, up there in that deep sanctuary area, where large numbers were being admitted to orders, something special was going on, but we probably understood little else.

Several years later, we gathered to celebrate orders at the cathedral church, the mother church of the diocese, because these men were being ordained to serve all of us in the diocese. As people grasped more and more deeply this sense of the diocesan church (the clarity of the vernacular was a help here), more and more people from all over the diocese joined in the prayer vigils that preceded these important events, and returned, rejoicing, to join in celebrating the culminating ritual.

Not to be overlooked here, when we consider orders, was the great gift within the church of the restoration of the permanent diaconate. The ordinations of these men, too, became high points in our understanding of church and of the way God uses the gifts of so many as chosen ministers of word and sacrament.

Year by year attendance at these celebrations grew, and participation became livelier. I recall explicitly the celebration in 1987 when Jack Thomas and Richard Smith were presented for orders. As the joyful sounds of the recessional carried the people forth, I knew the words of psalm forty-two in a new way:

> These things I remember,
> as I pour out my soul:
> how I went with the throng
> and led them in procession to the house
> of God,
> with glad shouts and songs of thanksgiving,
> a multitude keeping festival.

New joy in reconciliation

Archbishop Hayes invited priests and people to study the three forms of the new rite of reconciliation. I remember one rather lengthy session in which people posed question upon question. We all knew the experience of private auricular confession, but we had not experienced the possibilities that the new rite now offered. Education helped us understand and accept aspects of the new rite, such as going into a reconciliation room and talking to a priest face to face as we sought absolution, praying in common with other penitents and then, after seeking individual confession, coming together to pray our penance together, or, if the circumstances required it, receiving general absolution.

Archbishop Hayes encouraged us to be open to the different forms. It seemed that he felt the third form, which we had known for use only in times of war or disaster, was being offered to us for use at other times as well. Because we all had known how difficult it was, in an era of many priests, for both priests and people to experience reconciliation just prior to Christmas or Easter, we also knew that, in these days of fewer priests, it would be nearly impossible for a single priest to serve the members of even a few hundred families during those sacred days of preparation. And so, when the crowds arriving for this sacrament posed an impossible situation, our pastors were encouraged to make wise pastoral decisions in the matter. On these occasions the people found a new joy in this sacrament as they prayed and reflected together before they received absolution. Who had ever seen such joy in church following any other "confession" experience?

Renewal in the celebration of the
Chrism Mass and Triduum

No account such as this would be complete without reference to the change we experienced in our celebration of the Chrism Mass and of the night of the Easter Vigil, when the newly baptized are anointed with the holy oils. Although we had always known that the oils were blessed on Holy Thursday, it was only as we realized they were being blessed for us that our need to be there praying as the oils were consecrated became clearer.

Prior to Vatican II, very few people attended the Chrism Mass and little participation was expected from them. As I look back over the changes in the intervening years, however, I see the contrasts. The crowds have grown from year to year, made up of people from all over the diocese—groups who have been involved in working with candidates preparing for reception into the church, those to be baptized or received into full communion with the church at the Easter Vigil, those to be confirmed during the ensuing Pentecost season, along with many others.

I recall the first rumours of a move to celebrate the Easter Vigil in a way similar to the way it was celebrated in the early days of the church, when it was a night of prayer in anticipation of the Easter dawn. I recall a weekend diocesan workshop held around 1950 at Saint Mary's University, and led by an ardent liturgist, Jesuit William Leonard of Boston. It concluded with a demonstration of the rites of the Easter Vigil to help prepare us for what would lie ahead. The reforms of Vatican II brought further changes. Over time, the reform has given our celebrations a new tone. The assembly participates well because people know better what they are celebrating and are eager to be there. Under the continuing influence of the Rite of Christian Initiation of Adults, this celebration is still noticeably growing and effecting change in us.

Including women

Another gift James Hayes brought to many in the diocese is his sensitivity to the issue of inclusiveness of women. In his time as president of the Episcopal Commission for Liturgy, he exerted influence in this matter and, although this is still an area where more growth is desired, we find hope in the support of a friend.

Loved in our very weakness

Perhaps the dearest lesson Archbishop Hayes taught was to be unafraid in the face of a mistake. He said that, were we to fail in the midst of a liturgical celebration, we should pick ourselves up and go right on, knowing that our human frailty gave no offence to God, that we were loved in our very weakness. He did stress, however, the need for good and thorough preparation for any celebration.

Ministry to the sick

I believe we know James Hayes' love for the eucharist, not from written treatises or pious conversations or his telling others of such devotion, but rather from the way he lived his life in service of all of us in the church. He has spent himself for us. His ministry to the sick continues this pattern.[3]

Currently Archbishop Hayes devotes his time to ministry to the sick as chaplain at the Halifax Infirmary unit of the Camp Hill Medical Centre. He has always had a heart for the suffering and bereaved. In this latest channel of peace-giving, he continues to give his all, and is endearing himself to many. Once more, in this ministry, the man does not spare himself, but travels back and forth, after regular hours, to the bedside of the most vulnerable. He also supports families devastated as they must release their loved one to the Lord of all. I'm told that the sacrament of the sick has taken on a new meaning for them.

On September 15, 1993, at the annual mass offered in the small chapel of Our Lady of Sorrows in Holy Cross cemetery, Archbishop Hayes spoke to us of the ministry of consolation and later distributed copies of a paper in which he had researched the whole topic.[4] It was not a surprising gesture. His research indicates his way of approaching things from every angle, giving a sound and balanced outlook that blends both the intellectual and the human aspects of a topic.

Archbishop Hayes makes many a visit to our local funeral homes, because he sees the support of the bereaved as such an important ministry.

Presence to people at such times helps them weave into one tapestry all their previous encounters with the church, sacramental or otherwise. Sometimes it heals past hurts and it is always capable of deepening a bond with the church.

As I close these musings on the life and influence of James Martin Hayes on the church of Halifax, I am mindful of the description of the Old Testament prophet, Nehemiah. Because of his humanity to others and his willingness to trust in the God of his life, Nehemiah was able to be a moving force in the development of the spiritual life of the people of his time. James Hayes, in truth, could pray Nehemiah's prayer:

> Remember me, O my God, concerning this,
> and do not wipe out my good deeds
> that I have done for the house of my God
> and for his service.[5]

Notes

1. J. Brian Hanington, *Every Popish Person* (Archdiocese of Halifax: 1984), pp. 235-236.

2. *The Halifax Chronicle-Herald,* Feb. 12, 1965.

3. In an article in *Celebrate!* Vol. 32, No. 5, September-October 1993, Hayes writes, "To me, spending time with the dying person is like the experience of spending time before the blessed sacrament. The Lord is there and I am here. It means something to me and my faith tells me it means something to him. . . . It is different, somehow, from thinking about one another while engaged in some other activity. The church's liturgy for the care of the dying comes from an attitude like that." (p. 23)

4. *National Bulletin on Liturgy,* Vol. 26, # 132, Spring 1993, pp. 4-12.

5. Nehemiah 13:14.

The forty, the three and the fifty days: the paschal cycle in Augustine and Vatican II[1]

Joan Halmo

This article will summarize the thought of the Second Vatican Council on the paschal mystery, and then turn to writings of Augustine, one of the great fathers of the church. I will examine his understanding of the liturgical time-frame in which the church annually celebrates the Pasch: namely, the forty days of Lent, the three days known as the paschal triduum,[2] and the fifty days of Easter.

Archbishop James Hayes took part in the Second Vatican Council and, subsequently, has been a leader among those implementing its goals within the Canadian church. Generously and vigorously, he has carried out his commitment to one of the council's great ideals: the centrality of the paschal vision and the living of the paschal mission. He has fostered this paschal understanding in the church's life of worship and has promoted the renewal of Christian initiation. He has urged individual and corporate awareness of how "Pasch" translates into practical terms in the daily personal and communal life of today's followers of Jesus. For this work, he has integrated into his leadership the insights of theology, the call to spirituality and a sensitive awareness, particularly in the face of sickness and death, of the needs of pastoral care. In this way, his distinguished ecclesial service has embodied for our time ideals advanced centuries ago by Augustine. Here, then, are reflections on the paschal cycle, drawn, briefly, from the Second Vatican Council and, at greater length, from the fourth- and fifth-century thought of Hayes' fellow servant in the church, Augustine, Bishop of Hippo.

Paschal mystery: call to renewal in our time

Many of the Second Vatican Council's key documents emphasized that the paschal mystery is both the meaning of the mission of Jesus Christ and the heart of Christian life. The opening chapter of the *Constitution on the Sacred Liturgy* describes in paschal terminology the entire redemptive work of Jesus:

> Christ the Lord brought [this deed of human redemption and perfect glorification of God] to its completion, above all through the paschal mystery, that is, his passion, his resurrection from the dead and his glorious ascension. Through this, "in dying he destroyed our death; in rising he restored our life." For the tremendous sacrament which is the whole church arose from the side of Christ as he slept on the cross.[3]

Similarly, the paschal mystery is central to the life of the individual Christian in the world, and becomes the context in which all of life is lived. The council documents offer many rich passages written in this vein, among them:

> Christians are certainly subject to the need and duty to struggle against evil through many tribulations and to suffer death; but they share in the paschal mystery and are configured to the death of Christ, and so are strengthened in the hope of attaining to the resurrection.[4]

> Undergoing death on behalf of all of us sinners, [Jesus Christ] teaches us by his example the need to carry the cross which the flesh and the world lay upon those who pursue peace and justice. Established as lord by his resurrection and given all power in heaven and on earth, Christ is now at work in human hearts through the strength of his Spirit. . . .[5]

This strong and recurrent emphasis on Pasch is nowhere better seen than in the renewal related to the liturgical calendar. The latter highlights the paschal mystery in the church year, commencing, of course, with the Sunday, but also emphasizing the paschal mystery as celebrated in an annual festival. Prior to Vatican II, the 1955 restoration of the paschal vigil was a milestone in recognizing the primacy of the Pasch. This reform concentrated on the vigil itself, "the mother of all vigils," and the night of the great passover. Vatican Council II, affirming the vigil's centrality, took a giant step forward in reshaping the triduum as a cohesive liturgical unit. The triduum can thus reveal its richest meaning as a unitive time in honour of Jesus' dying, rising and glory. As the *General Norms* state it:

> Christ redeemed us all and gave perfect glory to God principally through his paschal mystery: dying he destroyed our death and rising he restored our life. Therefore the Easter triduum

of the passion and resurrection of Christ is the culmination of the entire liturgical year.[6]

Without doubt, the restored Rite of Christian Initiation of Adults (RCIA) gave impetus to the keeping of the entire paschal cycle. Closely linked in the church's early life to the shape, ritual, imagery and meaning of the paschal liturgical celebrations, the RCIA, in contemporary practice, has nurtured greatly the renewal of the local church's understanding and manner of celebrating the paschal cycle.[7]

The emergence of greater focus on the triduum and the paschal mystery that it celebrates has permitted the seasons surrounding the triduum to recover more of their authentic meaning. Vatican II presents the great fifty days of Easter as the time overflowing with the fullness of Christ's presence and the presence of his Spirit.[8] As in the early church, the season of the Fifty is regarded as a single entity, the Great Sunday. From beginning to end, the whole season is considered as the one day of the resurrection, the day made by the Lord, in which we rejoice and are glad. What is more, the now well-known experience of the restored mystagogia demonstrates that these days are a necessary unfolding of the Easter mystery for the newly-baptized in the midst of the church community.

The forty days, a time of preparation during which the community journeys together with the elect, can be best described as the preparation of both catechumens and faithful for the paschal mystery.[9] The Forty continues to be a period for the traditional practices of prayer, fasting and almsgiving. It is also a time of growth in spiritual health and wholeness, the time for Christians to do wholeheartedly what they should always do.[10]

The council's emphasis on the Pasch in liturgy, initiation and life became, and continues to be, a major part of the agenda for post-conciliar renewal. Clearly, much of the guidance in refurbishing our appreciation of the paschal cycle is rooted in the twentieth century's extensive liturgical and patristic scholarship; hence a study of early liturgical practices and patristic writings can only enrich our knowledge of the tradition to which we are heirs.

Among all the western fathers of the church, Augustine has the most copious and detailed works on the paschal cycle. In his thought, pastoral influences blend with a deep and encompassing spirituality, breadth of doctrinal teaching, liturgical insight and a poetic appreciation of the wonder of God's grace. His writings on the paschal cycle furnish an example of a great, unified liturgical theme embedded within a complex, effusive and fascinating mosaic of thought. Augustine sees the time spans as symbolic and significant in themselves: the forty lenten days, the central three days and, finally, the Easter fifty days. Exploring the biblical sources of these times, pondering their significance from various perspectives and savouring the depth of their many levels of meaning, the Christian comes to treasure not only the liturgical, but also the lived, paschal mystery.

The paschal cycle in sermons and a letter of Augustine

Lent: the forty days

For Augustine, the forty-day season of Lent is closely bound up with life in the world. This temporal association is inherent in the number forty itself. Turning to cosmological phenomena,

Augustine speaks of the four regions of the earth (Sermon 210:6, p. 104);[11] he refers to the four winds and the four seasons (Letter 55, p. 284).[12] Drawing on the scriptures, he points to the four channels through which Christ's gospel is spread to the four corners of the earth (Serm. 252:10, p. 335). Any of these multiplied by ten yields forty. And whence the ten? It refers to the decalogue—the ten commandments, which have been received and observed in all the four corners of the universe. The decalogue in turn represents life on earth under the law (Serm. 210:6, p. 104). In another scriptural connection, Augustine sees the number ten as representing the fullness of wisdom, which is given us for our sojourn in life, and "temporarily portioned out to us here [on earth]" (Serm. 252:10, p. 334). The number forty, then, as a multiple of four and ten, is bound up with things earthly, and shows Lent as representing a "life full of suffering in this mortal period of distress" (Serm. 243:9, p. 278; see also Serm. 210:4-5, pp. 101-3).

More important are the number forty's deep scriptural roots associated with the mighty Old Testament figures, Moses and Elijah. Both Moses, representing the law, and Elijah, the prophets, fasted forty days in connection with their God-given mission (Serm. 210:7, p. 105. See also Serm. 252:10, p. 334; Letter, p. 283). Above all, Jesus, who fulfils all that the law and the prophets foretold, fasted in the desert for forty days after his baptism (*ibid.*). Augustine underlines the nature of Jesus' fast as one occasioned by the "[anticipated] temptation of the Devil" (Serm. 210:2, p. 99). Likewise, the church's lenten fast is essentially a time of intense spiritual struggle with the tempter, a time of full Christian living in discipline and good works (*ibid.*). While

Augustine appears to equate Lent with fasting, it is obvious he means more than abstention from food; indeed, one may be prevented by personal circumstances from taking part in the corporal fast. Rather, an integrated and full lenten observance centres on fervent prayer and charity in the form of almsgiving and forgiveness (Serm. 210:8-10, p. 105ff).

Augustine carefully reiterates that the forty days are observed "at the approach of the solemnity of the Lord's Passion" (Serm. 210:1, p. 97; 210:3, p. 100; 210:5, p. 102). In so doing he moves toward another insight into the meaning of the forty days: the bridegroom's absence, a theme which, properly speaking, belongs specifically to the paschal celebration (i.e., triduum). "Because the bridegroom has been taken away," he writes, "we, the children of that beautiful bridegroom, certainly must mourn" (Serm. 210:3, p. 100). The idea of the bridegroom's departure is borrowed, as it were, and advanced from the three days of Pasch into the forty days of Lent, revealing the intimate link between them, and designating the Forty as spiritual preparation for the Three. Augustine weaves together these two images of Lent, that of the time of trial and of the bridegroom's absence: "this life in which we sojourn apart from him is full of temptations" (Serm. 210:5, p. 103). And subtly, almost unexpectedly, he leaps ahead in liturgical time and telescopes the meaning of Lent with the liturgical expression that the paschal triduum will give to the Lord's absence and anticipated return: we wait in the night (of this world of Lent, and of the paschal vigil as well) . . . " until the day dawns and the morning star rises in [our] hearts" (Serm. 210:5, p. 102-3).

Lent, then, signifies and embodies this life "where there is the utmost anxiety, where there is fear, where there are dangers from temptation" (Serm. 252:11, p. 335), when the bridegroom is not with us. How would the *ecclesia* liturgically express such a time? By fasting; by prayer of supplication; by omitting in its worship the "alleluia," that song belonging, not to this world, but to the world to come.

Pasch: the triduum

The point to which Lent moves and from which the fifty days of Easter take their departure is the Pasch, celebrated on three days as the central Christian feast of redemption. For Augustine, Pasch means "passage,"[13] and his discussion of the triduum on both the Christological and ecclesiological levels hinges on this concept of one great movement from death to life.

Augustine explains in his Letter to Januarius that the time chosen to celebrate the passage to new life is, fittingly, March, the first month of the year for the civilization of his time (Letter, p. 264). That the festival is three days long is linked with the symbolism of the number three: "truly, in the whole time of the world, the third period has now come, and therefore, the resurrection of the Lord happened on the third day" (Letter, p. 264). To explain, Augustine adds: "[the third period] is under grace, where we now have the revealing of a mystery previously hidden in prophetic obscurity" *(ibid.)*. In another reference to the significance of three, Augustine notes that the Pasch itself is celebrated in the third week of the moon. In all of these associations, the theme of newness recurs.

Among his considerations on the extended celebration of the Pasch over a period of three days,[14] Augustine comments on the placement of the feast to incorporate the Lord's day of rest. It is fitting, he writes, that the yearly Pasch include the sabbath of old because "we return through rest to that original life from which the soul fell into sin" (Letter, p. 274). That original life itself is now symbolized by the Lord's day, the Sunday, the eighth day with all its eschatological overtones. The celebration of the Pasch is comprised of "the three sacred days of his crucifixion, burial, resurrection . . . of these, the cross signifies what we do in this present life, but the burial and resurrection what we perform by faith and hope" (Letter, p. 279). Each of the three days is calculated, in the Jewish manner, from the night preceding it: the night (here, in a spiritual sense as well) and day of Jesus' death; the night beginning the sabbath rest and then the Sabbath itself; and finally, the night "which, in turn, belongs to the beginning of the Lord's Day, since the Lord consecrated it by the glory of His Resurrection" (Serm. 221:4, p. 178).

For the church of Augustine's time, the triduum was, then, the feast of the whole redemptive work of Christ: his suffering, death, and resurrection seen as one event, the Pasch. In his reflections on the paschal vigil, Augustine joins the apostle Paul in making this unity clear: we celebrate Christ who was delivered up for our sins, and rose again for our justification (Serm. 220, p. 173). The same thought wonderfully opens another vigil sermon:

> Since our Lord Jesus Christ made one day dolorous by His death and another glorious by his resurrection, let us, by recalling both days in solemn commemoration, keep vigil in memory of his death and rejoice in celebration of his resurrection. This is our yearly feast; it is our Passover, not symbolized by the slaying of an animal as in

the case of the ancient people, but fulfilled by the victim of salvation as to a new people, because "Christ, our Passover, has been sacrificed," and "the former things have passed away; behold, they are made new!" For us we do not mourn unless weighed down by our sins, nor do we rejoice unless justified by his grace, inasmuch as he "was delivered up for our sins, and rose again for our justification." In our grief over his death and our joy at his resurrection, we are happy; and because, on account of us and for our sake, sorrow was endured and joy anticipated, we do not proceed in ungrateful forgetfulness but we celebrate in grateful memory. (Serm. 221:1, p. 175)

Augustine further develops the meaning of the Pasch for the church: she too is in passage, "a passing from death to life, which begins by faith" (Letter, p. 264). The crucifixion is each Christian's death to sin, to the "old man" (Letter, pp. 279-280), a process begun in baptism, when we enter Christian existence. We are "brought into being by his death" (Serm. 236:1, p. 231), a death that also becomes ours. But the resurrection of Christ is also part of Pasch, and it is by the resurrection that "we come to maturity" (*ibid.*), and to "those things which we do not yet see, and do not yet hold, but which we grasp by faith and hope" (Letter, p. 281).

An image that we have met before returns: it is the figure of the bridegroom, here lightly, yet distinctly, etched. Christ died to give us sleepless life (Serm. 221:3, p. 177). Meanwhile, have we been sleeping, or have we kept watch—spiritually, during the Lent of our life, and now liturgically, at the vigil which will bring the triduum to a climax? While the bridegroom is away, sleeping in death, we should be awake, lamps in hand ... when he returns he will bring us who once slept in the death of sin to a life which knows neither sleep nor death! (Serm. 221:4, p. 177 ff.) The themes of light and darkness, so prominent in symbol at the vigil, here enter marvellously into Augustine's commentary: the night of our darkness is illumined by Christ himself, who is light and in whom we come from darkness to light (Serm. 221:1-4, p. 175 ff.).

Christ, Lord and bridegroom, returns from death to bring his waiting *ecclesia* light and life. He returns in sacramental presence that we perceive by faith. The "absence" of Christ (i.e., through his death and burial) during the first part of the great Pasch comes to an end with the liturgical celebration of the resurrection, in which the church too is reborn and enters into new life. The sacraments, especially of water, but also of spirit and table, are the visible signs of his presence among his people: "what truth declares has actually happened only once, this the solemnity renews . . ." (Serm. 220, p. 173). This abundance of new life, that of Christ and that of the church, is perceived only by faith—a theme to which Augustine will return repeatedly in his Easter season sermons.

Easter season: the fifty days

Having made the passage with Christ from death to new life, the *ecclesia* celebrates a joyous fifty days. Explaining the symbolism of the number fifty, Augustine recalls the forty days of lenten labour and then adds to these the number ten, derived etymologically from the *denarius*; he declares that their sum signifies the reward for labour here on earth (Serm. 210:6, p. 104; Serm. 252:11, p. 336). Referring to the Hebrew scriptures, he links the fifty days with the time between Israel's passover and the giving of the law, a type of the fifty days between Jesus' resurrection and the coming of the Spirit (Serm. 252:10, pp. 333-34; Letter, pp. 285-87). Yet another aspect of fifty is derived from the multiplication of seven by seven, with an addition of one for the fiftieth day; and "when there is a return to the beginning, which is the octave, identical with the first, fifty is complete" (Letter, p. 284). These allusions and images connected with fifty—the reward, the plenitude, the joy—characterize the Easter season as the time of fulfilment and completion.

For Augustine, the fifty days radiate such happiness because they are a taste of the blessedness of the life to come, the life into which Christ entered by his resurrection and the life he bestows upon his church. This eschatological dimension, with its "now" and "not-yet" aspects, is very much a part of the fabric of the Easter season. These "joyful days point to a future life where we are destined to reign with the Lord" (Serm. 243:9, p. 278). Unlike the lenten season, which represented a state of life the church not only observes but also possesses (i. e., temporality, with its labor and suffering), the Easter season brings joy which "we observe . . . but do not yet possess" (Serm. 254:5, pp. 345-46).

Since Christians still live in this world, the only way to experience the Lord's risen presence is by faith. Augustine returns to this as to a refrain throughout the Easter season sermons: whether commenting on the resurrection appearances of Christ, or encouraging Christians to live worthily, he urges faith: "Faith is demanded of us; salvation is offered to us . . . Precious is the gift which is promised to us; what is bidden [faith] is fulfilled without cost" (Serm. 233:1, p. 218, see also 228,

p. 200; 243:2, p. 273; Letter, p. 262 ff.; p. 281 ff.). In his explanation of John 21:6-11, he invites a faith-filled recognition of the risen Lord at work in his church at the present time: "Do we not see . . . that the Word of God is the net, that the world is the sea, and that all who believe are included within the net?" (Serm. 252:2, p. 326). Commenting on Mary Magdalene's meeting with the risen Christ, Augustine reveals most clearly the meaning of Easter faith for the *ecclesia:* "But what mortal can touch him when he is seated in heaven if he does not touch him here on earth?. . . That touch, moreover, signifies belief; he who believes in Christ, touches Christ" (Serm. 243: 1-2, p. 273).

Like Mary Magdalene, the church knows her risen Lord by faith, and her joy overflows. It is joy in the bridegroom's presence, the taste of a "rejoicing which no one will take from us" (Serm. 210:6, p. 104). The season's liturgical and spiritual practices are in complete contrast to those of Lent and appropriately express the gladness of Easter: there can be no fasting, for the Lord and bridegroom is risen and among us; no kneeling, but rather "we pray standing, which is a sign of resurrection" (Letter, p. 284).

Most of all, as its acknowledgment *par excellence* of resurrection, the church sings "Alleluia," "to indicate that our future occupation is to be no other than the praise of God" (Letter, p. 284; see also Serm. 210:6, p. 104; 228:1, p. 198; 243:9, p. 278; 252:9, pp. 332-3). "For what does 'Alleluia' mean?" asks Augustine. "It is a Hebrew word signifying 'praise God' and . . . by our 'Alleluia' . . . we arouse one another to praise God" (Serm. 243:9, p. 278). In this one word is crystallized the joy the church knows in the risen Christ, and the delights that will be hers fully when she enters the marriage feast of the Lamb in eternity:

> Then there will be "Alleluia" in reality; now, only in hope. Hope sings it, and love sings it now; love will also sing it then, but it will be a satisfied love while now it is a hungry love (Serm. 255:5, p. 353).

While still on earth, the pilgrim church could weary even of so marvellous a task, singing God's praise. But then, when the *ecclesia* shall have made her final passage into the full joy of resurrection, when she will have seen her bridegroom face to face, all weariness will be past. She shall stand in the house of God and give praise forever and ever (Serm. 243:9, p. 279).

Notes

1. The original idea for the topic of this paper came from Patrick Regan, O.S.B., Abbey of St. Joseph, St. Benedict, Louisiana; and the suggestion that this reflection become my tribute in this collection for Archbishop Hayes, from Dr. Walter Kreyszig, University of Saskatchewan, Saskatoon, Saskatchewan, and University of Vienna, Austria. I am grateful to them both, as also to Dr. Frank Henderson, University of Alberta, Edmonton, for his thoughts on the paschal cycle in contemporary times.

2. In the translation into English of *General Norms for the Liturgical Year and the Calendar* (Rome: 1969), the Latin *triduum paschale* was rendered as "Easter triduum"; see General Norms, nn. 18-19, *Documents of the Liturgy 1963-1979: Conciliar, Papal, and Curial Texts*, prepared by the International Commission on English in the Liturgy (Collegeville, Minnesota: Liturgical Press, 1982). The term *paschale*, with its rich scriptural and liturgical dimensions, when given as "Easter," focuses primarily on resurrection; this translation does not enhance the understanding of the three days as a comprehensive celebration of the entire paschal mystery.

3. Vatican Council II, *Constitution on the Sacred Liturgy*, no. 5. This translation, as others from the Council documents, is cited from *Decrees of the Ecumenical Councils*, Volume II, Trent – Vatican II, ed. Norman P. Tanner, S.J. (London: Sheed and Ward and Washington: Georgetown University Press, 1990).

4. Vatican Council II, *Pastoral Constitution on the Church in the Modern World*, 1, 22.

5. *Ibid.*, 3, 38.

6. *General Norms*, n. 18.

7. As this brief paper focuses on the significance of the Forty, the Three and the Fifty days in relationship to each other and on their meaning as related to scriptural passages, little is included here in regard to Christian initiation as an important part of the paschal cycle, although the church of Hippo at Augustine's time, like others of the day, enshrined initiation within the cycle of the liturgical year. Augustine certainly alludes to initiation in specific addresses to the catechumens (especially Sermons 205-16), and through numerous references to paschal baptism (e.g., Sermon 210) and to the newly-baptized (e.g., Sermon 228). The Letter to Januarius is more preoccupied with an understanding of the whole paschal cycle and of the implications of the paschal mystery in the life of the individual Christian.

8. *General Norms*, n. 22

9. *Ibid.*, n. 27

10. *Circular Letter Concerning the Preparation and Celebration of the Easter Feasts* (Rome, 1988) contains greater detail on liturgical aspects of the paschal cycle than the Vatican II documents provided. See the *National Bulletin on Liturgy* 22, no. 116 (1989), 51-68. The circular letter essentially assembles and organizes liturgical norms already in existence.

11. All translations of the sermons of Augustine are taken from *The Fathers of the Church*, gen. ed. Roy Joseph Deferrari, vol. 38: *Saint Augustine–Sermons on the Liturgical Seasons*, trans. Mary Sarah Muldowney (New York: Fathers of the Church, Inc., 1959). Page numbers are indicated in the references for ease of locating texts. For Augustine's sermons in the Latin original, see Jacques Paul Migne, ed., *Patrologiae cursus completus, Series latina* [PL] 38 (Paris: D'Ambroise, 1841).

12. The translation of the "Letter to Januarius" is from *The Fathers of the Church*, gen. ed. Roy Joseph Deferrari, vol. 12: *Saint Augustine–Letters*, vol. 1, trans. Wilfrid Parsons (New York: Fathers of the Church, Inc., 1951). For the original Latin text of the "Letter to Januarius," see *PL* 33 (1886).

13. Another aspect included in the term Pasch is that of the passion, as explained by Melito of Sardis in a second-century homily: "What is the Pasch? Its name is derived from the verb 'to suffer,' to be suffering. . ." See Melito, "Paschal Homily," trans.

Thomas Halton, *The Paschal Mystery, Ancient Liturgies and Patristic Texts,* ed. A. Hamman (Staten Island, N.Y.: Alba House, 1969), p. 31. Augustine places more stress on the dimension of passing-over, the passage.

14. In Augustine's time, the three days were in actuality that, comprised of Friday, Saturday, and Sunday, while Thursday preceding the triduum was still very much the last day of Lent and not part of the triduum.

Fulfilled in our hearing: the dynamism of scripture in liturgical proclamation

Normand Bonneau, O.M.I.

The Vatican II revision of the *Sunday and Feast Day Lectionary* aimed to restore the liturgical proclamation of scripture to the prominence it had enjoyed in the early church. In the final analysis the thorough reform of the lectionary may well emerge as the most spectacular and far-reaching of all the liturgical reforms inspired by the council.[1]

The heightened profile of scripture in the reformed liturgy—a three-year cycle of readings, three readings per Sunday and feast day, the introduction of the Old Testament as a standard feature—has prompted renewed interest in the role of the bible in worship. The 1969 *Introduction to the Lectionary for Mass* and the expanded *Introduction* to the 1981 edition have been designed to elucidate the function of scriptural proclamation in liturgy and to describe the principles underlying the selection and distribution of biblical passages. In addition, a growing body of literature recounts how the revision of the lectionary was accomplished and evaluates the strengths and weaknesses of the final product.[2]

One of the issues that arises in the discussion of the lectionary—one that, in particular, elicits critiques from some scripture scholars—is the lectionary's way of selecting biblical passages with little concern for their original context.[3] This tendency stems from the fact that the Sunday and feast day lectionary is first and foremost a liturgical book. As such, it is totally oriented to the paschal mystery of Christ's death and resurrection.[4] Since liturgy is an action making present this saving mystery,[5] all the scripture readings in the lectionary are selected to express and accompany the action being celebrated. Christian liturgy has always felt free to select and use texts according to its needs.[6] As a result, liturgical settings invest biblical texts with interpretations at times quite foreign to their original intent. Does this tendency to decontextualize biblical excerpts distort or do violence to the scriptures?

The aim of this article is to show that the lectionary, both in its selection and in its distribution of biblical passages, rather than distorting or doing violence to the scriptures, in fact continues the dynamism inherent in the scriptures themselves. A comparison between the Sunday lectionary's use of the gospels and the history of gospel formation will illustrate how this dynamism, detectable throughout the lectionary, works.

A first step will examine the salient characteristics of the lectionary's selection and distribution of gospel passages, both in festal seasons and in ordinary time. The second step will provide a sketch of the genesis of the gospels. Finally, a rapprochement between the two will point out how the lectionary continues the dynamic trajectory initiated in the earliest gospel tradition.

A. Gospel passages in the Sunday lectionary

The post-Vatican II *Sunday and Feast Day Lectionary* is a highly selective and carefully structured repertoire of biblical passages distributed over a three-year cycle. The gospels maintain pride of place in this revised lectionary, for one of its most distinctive hallmarks is the assigning of a synoptic gospel to each year, Matthew to Year A, Mark to Year B, and Luke to Year C.

An examination of two sequences of gospel readings, one from the festal season of Lent, the other from Ordinary Time, demonstrates how the Sunday lectionary removes passages from their original story lines and re-situates them in a liturgical narrative.

1. Gospels for Lent

The liturgical year comprises two kinds of seasons, festal seasons (Advent, Christmas, Lent, Easter) and Ordinary Time. The lectionary marks this distinction by employing different principles of reading selection and reading distribution for each type of season. The characteristic principle of the festal seasons is harmony, whereby certain biblical books or parts of books are selected to articulate the main themes of the season. For the Sundays in Ordinary Time, the lectionary distributes the gospel passages according to the principle of semicontinuous reading. This modern adaptation of the ancient practice of *lectio continua* offers a significant exposure to a biblical book by selecting excerpts in their original sequence, all the while skipping intervening chapters or verses.

The gospel passages for the first five Sundays of Lent, like the gospels for all the festal seasons, are chosen to articulate the themes of the season. The *General Norms for the Liturgical Year and the Calendar* (no. 27) specifies these themes:

> Lent is a preparation for the celebration of Easter. For the Lenten liturgy disposes both catechumens and the faithful to celebrate the paschal mystery: catechumens, through the several stages of Christian initiation; the faithful, through reminders of their own baptism and through penitential practices.

In Year A, the gospel excerpts which the lectionary offers for Lent focus primarily on the candidates for initiation. Proceeding from the first to the fifth Sunday, the readings are: Matthew 4:1-11, the temptation of Jesus; Matthew 17:1-9, the transfiguration; John 4:5-42, the Samaritan woman at the well; John 9:1-41, the man born blind; and John 11:1-45, the raising of Lazarus.

The temptation and the transfiguration, proclaimed on the first and second Sundays respectively, function as an overture to the entire Lent-Easter cycle. They are selected to evoke the key facets of Jesus' paschal mystery, his passion, death and resurrection. By epitomizing his struggle against sinfulness in all its guises, the temptation conjures up Jesus' suffering and death. The episode already hints at Jesus' ultimate triumph, for he does not succumb to Satan's enticements. The transfiguration adumbrates the resurrection. Following immediately upon Jesus' passion prediction, the account intimates that Jesus' journey to Jerusalem to face suffering and death will lead to glorification.

Thus the two opening lenten gospels present the essential pattern of the paschal mystery—the passage through death to new life—into which the candidates are configured by passing through the waters of baptism at the Easter Vigil.

The long narratives from John's gospel, read on the third, fourth and fifth Sundays of Lent, Year A, are specifically oriented to the catechumens. The liturgy pairs these readings with the scrutinies. Originally exorcisms, the scrutinies have been reformulated as prayers through which the assembly beseeches God to make the candidates open and receptive to the transformation they are to experience in their upcoming baptism. In this setting, the passages from John 4, 9, and 11 recount what happens when someone meets the risen Lord: they offer models by which the candidates can interpret their own experience of coming to faith. Initiation into the paschal mystery means "passing over" from sin to grace (John 4), from darkness to light (John 9), from death to life (John 11). This felicitous marriage of the readings from John with the scrutinies revives an ancient tradition reaching back to the fourth century.

Clearly, then, the gospel readings for the first five Sundays of Lent, Year A, are removed from their original narrative contexts. Indeed, set within the lenten liturgy, these passages relate only incidentally to their original gospel story lines, for the lectionary selects them and embeds them in a new narrative provided by the liturgical action being celebrated: the candidates' journey to faith and conversion.

Each festal season stresses a particular aspect of the Jesus story as celebrated by the worshipping assembly. Lent's story of conversion and repentance culminates in the believers' appropriation of the paschal mystery through baptism and eucharist at the Easter Vigil. The triduum initiates the candidates and intensifies the faithful's participation in this central mystery of faith. The Easter season celebrates the story of the deepening communion of the faithful with the risen Lord who abides with his church through the Spirit. The Advent-Christmas season unfolds the story of the community's patient waiting for the fullness of the kingdom still to come, a time of anticipation that they fill with purposeful action until the consummation of the paschal mystery is revealed in them.

In each instance, the gospel readings selected for the festal seasons articulate and celebrate these overarching liturgical narratives, for the purpose of the liturgy is to shape the assembly of believers into the body of the risen Christ. Nevertheless, although the liturgical narratives take precedence over the plotted gospel narratives, the two are intimately related. The liturgical narratives are inspired by and configured according to the narratives first recounted in the scriptures themselves. Conversion, repentance, communion, discipleship—it was to make present these same fundamental realities of Christian life that the gospels were first written.

2. The gospels during the Sundays in Ordinary Time

For the Sundays in Ordinary Time the lectionary arranges the synoptic gospels according to the principle of semicontinuous reading. In this way, "as the Lord's life and preaching unfold, the teaching proper to each of these gospels is presented" (*Introduction to the Lectionary for Mass* [1981], no. 105). Yet even here a significant degree of decontextualization occurs. The following sample of gospel passages—selections from the 23rd to the 30th Sundays in Ordinary Time, Year A—is a case in point. The table on page 125 lists all the pericopes between Matthew 18:15 and 22:40 so as to capture the flow of Matthew's story. The boldface entries indicate the passages included in the lectionary.

Most worshippers attending Sunday liturgy, unless they are very familiar with Matthew's gospel, will not notice that between the twenty-fifth and twenty-sixth Sundays, for example, the lectionary passes over a huge block of material crucial to Matthew's story line. Between the parable of the workers in the vineyard, read on the twenty-fifth Sunday, and the parable of the two sons, read on the twenty-sixth Sunday, Jesus has arrived in Jerusalem and cleansed the temple. In response, the chief priests and elders of the people confront him, asking where he received the authority to do such things. Jesus answers their challenge with three parables: the parable of the two sons, the parable of the vineyard, and the parable of the wedding banquet.

All three parables are noteworthy for the harshness of their message, readily understandable in the Matthean story line because Jesus aims them at his adversaries. During the Sundays in Ordinary Time, however, the lectionary skips over the triumphal entry and the cleansing of the temple, removing the immediate reason for the sting in Jesus' subsequent teaching. Although the lectionary tries to mitigate the loss of context by introducing the three parables with an *incipit* ("Jesus said to the chief priests and the elders of the people" and the like), they have been loosed from their narrative moorings. Preachers in fact usually apply the

23rd Sunday: Matthew 18:15-20. Forgive the brother or sister who sins against you; whatever you bind on earth will be bound in heaven. . .; where two or three are gathered in my name. . .

24th Sunday: Matthew 18:21-35. How often must I forgive?. . . The parable of the unforgiving servant
> Matthew 19:1-12. On marriage and divorce.
> Matthew 19:13-15. "Let the little children come unto me."
> Matthew 19:16-30. The rich young man.

25th Sunday: Matthew 20:1-16. The parable of the workers in the vineyard.
> Matthew 20:17-19. The third passion prediction.
> Matthew 20:20-28. The sons of Zebedee ask to sit on the Lord's right and left in the kingdom.
> Matthew 20:29-34. Jesus heals two blind men.
> Matthew 21:1-9. Jesus' triumphal entry into Jerusalem.
> Matthew 21:10-17. Jesus' cleansing of the temple.
> Matthew 21:18-22. The cursing of the fig tree.
> Matthew 21:23-27. The chief priests and the elders of the people question Jesus about his authority to cleanse the temple.

26th Sunday: Matthew 21:28-32. The parable of the two sons.

27th Sunday: Matthew 21:33-43. The parable of the vineyard.
> Matthew 21:45-46. The chief priests and the elders of the people try to arrest Jesus.

28th Sunday: Matthew 22:1-14. The parable of the wedding banquet.

29th Sunday: Matthew 22:15-21. The debate regarding tribute to Caesar.
> Matthew 22:22-33. Debate with Sadducees on resurrection.

30th Sunday: Matthew 22:34-40. The greatest commandment.

parables to the assembled community as though Jesus had aimed them at his disciples rather than at his adversaries. The worshipper is led to ponder, "Am I the obedient or the disobedient son?" "Am I producing fruits of the kingdom?" "Am I responding to the invitation to the king's banquet?" Such an interpretation is liturgically sound, because the liturgical narrative celebrated during the Sundays of the year is discipleship, a time devoted to apprenticeship for the kingdom.

In the Sundays in Ordinary Time, as in the Sundays in the festal seasons, the liturgy removes the gospel pericopes from their original contexts and makes them serve the new narrative it provides. The lectionary's propensity to decontextualize and to recontextualize gospel passages is nothing new, however, for in their formation the gospels themselves bear evidence of having undergone a similar process.

B. The formation of the gospels

An important legacy of modern historical-critical exegesis is the delineation of the history of gospel formation. Although some particulars are still debated, the majority of biblical scholars the world over and across confessional lines accepts the overall picture.

The gospels came to be in three stages: "(I) what Jesus of Nazareth did and said (corresponding roughly to A.D. 1-33); (II) what disciples preached about him, his words, and his deeds (corresponding roughly to A.D. 33-65); and (III) what evangelists wrote about him, having culled, synthesized, and explicated the tradition that preceded them, each in his own way (corresponding to A.D. 65-90)."[7] The exegetical method called form criticism deals with Stage II, while redaction criticism studies Stage III.

1. Stage II: Form criticism

Form criticism can be defined as "a systematic, scientific, historical, and theological methodology for analyzing the forms, and to some extent the content, of the primitive Christian literature, with special reference to the history of the early Christian movement in its reflective and creative theological activities."[8] Form criticism studies discrete pieces of tradition—*forms* such as sayings, parables, pronouncement stories, miracle stories, etc. Out of these building blocks the gospels were fashioned.

Form criticism is founded on several presuppositions, three of which are especially germane for comparison with the lectionary.[9] (1) "Before the Gospels were written there was a period of oral tradition." (2) "During the oral period, the narratives and sayings, with the exception of the passion narrative, circulated mainly as single and self-contained, detached units, each complete in itself." Forms—the earliest pieces of gospel tradition—first existed devoid of a written, narrative context.[10] (3) "The vital factors that gave rise to and preserved these forms are to be found in the practical interests of the Christian community." Among these practical interests, the most important were the kerygmatic, catechetical and liturgical exigencies of daily life in the early church. German biblical scholars coined the phrase *Sitz im Leben*, or "life settings," to refer to such Stage II situations in which the first Christian generation applied and actualized the gospel message.

2. Stage III: Redaction criticism

Redaction criticism examines Stage III of the gospel tradition, a stage later in the first century when the traditions, originally oral, were then committed to writing.[11] Robert Stein defines this method as "the study of NT texts that concentrates on the unique theological emphases that the writers place upon the materials they used, their specific purposes in writing their works, and the *Sitz im Leben* out of which they wrote."[12]

It is probable that, before they were incorporated into the gospels, some of these traditions had been written down and handed on in the form of small collections of sayings and stories. The narrative genre *gospel* in which they were finally embedded, however, remains the work of the evangelists. These authors, responsible for assembling and editing the forms of the tradition into plotted narratives, contextualized the individual stories and collections of stories into the gospels as we have them.

Despite their fundamental similarities, the four canonical gospels tell the story of Jesus in significantly different ways. Redaction criticism accounts for this by postulating that each evangelist tailored his gospel to respond to the needs of a particular community. Situated at Stage III of the development of the tradition, the four canonical gospels represent the actualizing and applying of the Jesus story to four different "life settings" or *Sitze im Leben* of the church during the last third of the first century.[13]

This admittedly simplified sketch highlights two essential dimensions of the dynamic process of gospel formation: (1) the relationship between the earliest units of gospel tradition and the later narrative contexts in which they were embedded is a contingent one, for the four evangelists used forms and collections of material in different ways; (2) after the resurrection, believers not only remembered the words and deeds of Jesus but also shaped and adapted them to meet their present needs of actualization.

C. Lectionary: the dynamism of scripture at work

The dynamic process that underlies the formation of the gospels continues in the liturgy. In its own way, the liturgy activates the process of recontextualizing and actualizing, as Robert Taft explains:

> ... the liturgy is the ongoing *Sitz im Leben* of Christ's saving pattern in every age, and what we do in the liturgy is exactly what the New Testament itself did with Christ: it applied him and what he was and is to the present. For the *Sitz im Leben* of the Gospels is the historical setting not of the original event, but of its telling during the early years of the primitive Church .... It is up to each generation to do what the Apostolic Church did in the very composition of the New Testament: apply the mystery of Christ to the *Sitz im Leben* of today."[14]

It is noteworthy that Taft employs the phrase *Sitz im Leben*, an exegetical term describing an important dimension of gospel formation, to account for what happens in the liturgy. The only codicil to add to Taft's words is that the lectionary eminently accomplishes this task of the liturgy.

The lectionary use of the gospels and the process of gospel formation are essentially the same. The lectionary decontextualizes gospel passages from their narrative settings, rendering them analogous to the way they existed in Stage II of gospel formation,[15] only to recontextualize them in another narrative. The liturgy, in applying the Jesus tradition to living communities of faith, provides this new narrative.

In its concern to actualize the mystery of salvation for the community here and now assembled, the liturgy also proceeds in a manner similar to that of the early stages of gospel formation. Both in Stage II and in Stage III the first Christian generations adapted the gospel tradition they inherited to respond to new times and situations. The recently published document of the Pontifical Biblical Commission on the interpretation of the bible in the church points out that this dynamism has endured throughout the ages: "It is the living tradition of the community of faith that stimulates the task of actualization. This community places itself in explicit continuity with the communities which gave rise to Scripture and which preserved and handed it on. In the process of actualization, tradition . . . ensures the transmission of the original dynamism."[16]

Although the liturgy does not produce gospel texts as did the early Christians, the dialogue it enables between the ancient scriptures and the present community of faith causes the gospel once again to become event in the lives of the assembled believers. The worshipping community, as it were, writes itself into the text; in turn the text generates new meaning by being confronted with the assembly's life settings at that specific juncture in salvation history.[17] In the final analysis, the gospel is not words on a page, but the saving presence of the risen Lord in the lives of the faithful. The liturgy's ability to transform the words of the text into the presence of the Word has always made liturgy the locus *par excellence* for experiencing the vitality of the scriptural tradition in the church.

Conclusion

What is said here about the lectionary's use of the gospels embraces the lectionary's use of scripture generally. It is the liturgical proclamation of the word, as configured in the lectionary, that activates the dynamism inherent in the scriptures themselves. Rather than distorting the scriptures, liturgy makes the scriptures fully what they are, the word of God present and active: "My word, says the Lord, shall not return to me empty, but it shall accomplish that which I purpose, and succeed in the thing for which I sent it" (Isaiah 55:11). Just as Luke portrays Jesus realizing in himself the ancient Isaian prophecy at the synagogue in Nazareth, so today the liturgical proclamation of scripture fulfils in our hearing the presence of the risen Christ (Luke 4: 21).[18]

Notes

1. Adrien Nocent, "La parole de Dieu et Vatican II," in Pierre Jounel, Reiner Kaczynski, Gottardo Pasqualetti, eds., *Liturgia, opera divina e umana: studi sulla riforma liturgica offerti a S. E. Mons. Annibale Bugnini in occasione del suo 70e compleanno* (Bibliotheca Ephemerides Liturgicae, Subsidia 26; Roma, CLV: Edizioni liturgiche, 1982), p. 141.

2. For an extensive list of such titles, see Fritz West, "An Annotated Bibliography on the Three-year Lectionaries. Part I: The Roman Catholic Lectionary," *Studia Liturgica* 23 (1993), pp. 223-44.

3. For example, Marie-Josèphe Rondeau, "Les évangiles dans le lectionnaire du dimanche," *Les quatre fleuves* 21-22 (1985), pp. 95-107. Also, A. Nocent, "La parole de Dieu et Vatican II," p. 138.

4.   "The lectionary was not to be ordered around a 'history of salvation' motif (understood as a line running from the creation to the second coming), or around a systematic presentation of the theological teachings of the church, or according to a literary analysis of the parts of the Bible that were to be used. Nor were the readings to be chosen and ordered for the primary purpose of exhorting and encouraging people to lead more Christian lives. The lectionary was there to proclaim the passion, death, resurrection, and ascension of Christ, fully realized in him and being realized in us who, through faith and baptism, have been joined to him." W. Skudlarek, *The Word in Worship* (Nashville: Abingdon, 1981), pp. 33-34.

5.   I. H. Dalmais, "Theology of the Liturgical Celebration," in I. H. Dalmais et al., eds., *Principles of the Liturgy* (The Church at Prayer: An Introduction to the Liturgy, Vol 1. Trans. Matthew O'Connell. Collegeville: The Liturgical Press, 1987), p. 229.

6.   ". . . toute tradition liturgique, au fil des siècles, s'est toujours sentie libre de choisir, de disposer, de rapprocher, d'interpréter et d'utiliser l'Ecriture comme une réalité qui lui appartient de par sa condition même. . ." Achille M. Triacca, "Bible et Liturgie," in Domenico Sartore et Achille M. Triacca, eds., *Dictionnaire Encyclopédique de la Liturgie*, Vol. 1 (A-L). (French adaptation under the direction of Henri Delhougne. Turnhout, Belgique: Brépols / Montréal: Sciences et culture, 1992), p. 143. "La Bible appartient en propre non pas à l'individu mais à l'Eglise. . . . Le choix et l'ordre des lectures bibliques est soumis à l'année ecclésiastique et aux fins de l'Eglise." Evangelos Theodorou, "La phénoménologie des relations entre l'Eglise et la liturgie," in A. M. Triacca and A. Pistola, eds., *L'Eglise dans la liturgie: Conférences Saint-Serge, XXVIe semaines d'études liturgiques. Paris, 26-29 juin, 1979* (Roma: Edizioni Liturgiche, 1980), p. 279.

7.   Joseph A. Fitzmyer, "Historical Criticism: Its Role in Biblical Interpretation and Church Life," *Theological Studies* 50 (1989), p. 252.

8.   W. G. Doty, *Contemporary New Testament Interpretation* (Englewood Cliffs, NJ: 1972), p. 62, as cited in Vernon K. Robbins, "Form Criticism (NT)," in David Noel Freedman, ed., *The Anchor Bible Dictionary*, Vol. 2 (New York: Doubleday, 1992), p. 841.

9.   Robert H. Stein, *The Synoptic Problem: An Introduction* (Grand Rapids: Baker Book House, 1987), p. 185. Even though these presuppositions have been refined in recent studies, their basic thrust remains.

10. A rapid look at the synoptic gospels confirms that this is so. For example, Mark 2:1-3:6 contains a series of controversy stories, all of which could exist independently; Mark 4:1-34 gathers a number of parables, each of which Jesus most probably preached at different times and places. Similar observations can apply to Matthew 5-7, the Sermon on the Mount, which lists several dozens of Jesus' sayings and teachings.

11. Stein uses the word inscripturation to describe this committing to writing of the earlier oral gospel tradition, *The Synoptic Problem*, p. 229.

12. Robert H. Stein, "Redaction Criticism, New Testament," in David Noel Freedman, ed., *The Anchor Bible Dictionary*, Vol. 5 (New York: Doubleday, 1992), p. 647.

13. This reapplying of earlier traditions to new circumstances is not unique to the gospels. It appears in numerous instances throughout the bible: "In the course of the Bible's formation, the writings of which it consists were in many cases reworked and reinterpreted so as to make them respond to new situations previously unknown." The Pontifical Biblical Commission, "The Interpretation of the Bible in the Church," *Origins* 23/29 (Jan. 6, 1994), p. 515.

14. Robert Taft, "The Liturgical Year: Studies, Prospects, Reflections," *Worship* 55 (1981), pp. 16-17, 22.

15. In the lectionary, the gospel pericopes are only analogously like the discrete pieces of gospel tradition on Stage II. As they exist in the lectionary the passages bear the marks of Stage III redactional activity of the gospel writers.

16. The Pontifical Biblical Commission, "The Interpretation of the Bible in the Church," p. 520.

17. Louis-Marie Chauvet, "What Makes the Liturgy Biblical?— Texts," *Studia Liturgica* 22 (1992), p. 128.

18. CSL no. 7: "He is present in his word, in that he himself is speaking when scripture is read in church."

Celebration: the Christian community responds to sickness and death

Corbin Eddy

Situated in the ritual, even before the *Apostolic Constitution* of Paul VI[1] and the *General Introduction to the Rites of Anointing*,[2] is a decree issued by the Congregation for Divine Worship.[3] Its opening sentence places all that follows in context:

> When the church cares for the sick, it serves Christ himself in the suffering members of his Mystical Body.

The decree then invites the community to proclaim, celebrate, and live out what it sees in the person of a suffering member. It invites the sick person to accept and embrace more fully this relationship with Christ that the church affirms. The decree continues, describing an adaptable complexus of prayers and activities with which the community of faith surrounds the sick person in times of special need.[4] The community and its ministers are called to respond sensitively to the uniqueness of the person.

Whatever is said and done must be appropriate and affirming as it seeks, in the power of the Spirit, to draw the sick, aging or dying person more deeply into the mystery of the incarnation of God in Christ.

It may be that the person needs patience and endurance as she waits for healing and recovery, so that she might be restored to her family and to her responsibilities within the broader community. It may mean that at a certain point the person is fighting the whole world and even God, as he or she struggles to deal with humanity, vulnerability, mortality. "Unfinished business" may surface in times of weakness and distress, crying out for inner healing or reconciliation. The person's loneliness simply may call for the presence of another believer in faithful support. Perhaps the person is calling for just a crumb of the eucharistic bread or a drop of eucharistic wine, pilgrim's food and drink, as she prepares to breathe her last. Assurance of safe passage from this world to the next. Assurance of real communion with Christ whose body is broken for her and whose blood is poured out for her. A new and everlasting covenant for the forgiveness of sins. An everlasting sign of God's fidelity. Her last breath: an "Amen" to this mystery.

All of this invites the sick person to respond in faith, to live this experience of suffering in communion with Christ so that "through him, with him, and in him, in the unity of the Holy Spirit, all glory and honour" be given to the Father. The General Instruction expresses these same foundational values: "Suffering and illness have always been among the greatest problems that trouble the human spirit. Christians feel and experience pain as do all other people; yet their faith helps them to grasp more deeply the mystery of suffering and to bear their pain with greater courage. From Christ's words they know that sickness has meaning and value for their own salvation and for the salvation of the world. They also know that Christ, who during his life often visited and healed the sick, loves them in their illness."[5]

An experience of faith proclaimed together

At the core of this approach to the sacraments is not a question of static objective "content" that is merely applied to a person in need, but an experience of faith that the suffering person and the community proclaim and celebrate together under unique circumstances. All believers know from experience that even the simple acts of anointing with oil or sharing the eucharist feel different and function differently in varying circumstances. The eucharist does not always taste the same. The sacrament of reconciliation graces us differently at various stages of our lives.

Constant, however, is the ongoing presence of Christ in his "church-body" and in its ongoing gracious proclamation, celebration and living out of that presence. Sin, sickness, old age or death are not the issues, as if they had some disembodied reality. Rather, sinful persons, sick persons, aging persons, dying persons and communities struggling to support these wounded members—and one another—proclaim and celebrate "life and light" in the liturgy.[6] The focus centres on the sick person and on the community surrounding him or her.

A paradox: celebration

In discussing the theme of festivity, and by extension the celebration of the sacraments, Joseph

Pieper notes the paradox involved in using this kind of terminology in reference to the celebration of a funeral, All Souls Day or Good Friday.[7] In providing an overall context, he refers to the tradition of scholastic philosophy for a reasonable framework. He reminds his readers that celebration involves an expression of joy, and that no one can rejoice absolutely for "joy's sake alone." Even the longing for happiness is the longing for a *reason* to be happy. This reason, to the extent that it exists, *precedes* joy and is different from it. The reason comes first; the joy comes second, and the reason for joy, though it may have a thousand facets, is always the same: experiencing what one loves.

As Pieper narrows his focus to the celebration of certain moments or events, he points out the incongruity of celebrating any particular moment if one cannot celebrate the whole of human life. Unless life as a whole is good, celebrating the birth of a child or the marriage of a daughter would have no meaning or substance. To have joy in any moment, one must be prepared for the possibility of joy in every moment. To say "Amen" at any given time involves the readiness to say "Amen" at every given time, however difficult that might be. It is a question of recognizing the rich possibilities of possessing that which is loved in good times and in bad, of being ready to discover rich and wonderful possibilities in life itself, even in all of its ambiguity.[8]

How would any of this be possible apart from religious faith? How could we celebrate the whole of life, including its most difficult moments, without reference to God, life's creative and unifying principle? Within the biblical tradition, the theme of God's covenant gives us a key that enables us to respond: God is absolutely faithful "in good times

and in bad, in sickness and in health—all our days."
In this covenant fidelity, proclaimed and ritualized
in all sacramental celebrations, the community and
its individual members experience themselves as
"possessing the Beloved"—the living God and
Father of our Lord Jesus Christ.[9]

Peter Berger, the sociologist of religion, and
Harold Kushner, rabbi and best-selling author,
approach the same question from different points of
view, but come to the same fundamental
conclusions. Commenting on a mother's
reassurance to her child who awakens in the night
from a bad dream, "Everything is all right," Berger
says: ". . . this common scene raises a far-from-
ordinary question which immediately introduces a
religious dimension: *Is the mother lying to her child?*
The answer can be No only if there is some truth to
the religious interpretation of human existence. . . .
The reassurance, transcending the immediately
present two individuals and their situation, implies
a statement about reality as such."[10]

Kushner, from his perspective, notes: "Religion
is not primarily a set of beliefs, a collection of
prayers, or a series of rituals. Religion is first and
foremost a way of seeing. It can't change the facts
about the world we live in, but it can change the way
we see those facts, and that in itself can often make
a real difference."

Acknowledging that two people visiting the
same hospital corridor may perceive vastly different
realities, Kushner asks, "The facts are the same for
each of us, but do we really see the same thing?"

One person will conclude that "the world is a
mess and life is Somebody's idea of a nasty joke. . .".
Another person will conclude, from the same
realities, "that incurable illnesses are a painful

outrage *precisely because* life is good and holy. Otherwise why would it grieve us so much when a life is cut short? For her, the courage to love in the face of the world's unfairness is the most profoundly human response."[11]

God's unconditional love

Each in its own way, the sacraments of reconciliation, anointing and eucharist involve a renewed sealing in the covenant of God's unconditional love for people and of Christ's unconditional love for the church. The sacraments affirm and ritualize the Christian's call to communion with Christ in good times and in bad.

It is not difficult to see how personal piety can be integrated with, and enriched by, the church's liturgical spirituality. In a real sense, they feed off each other. It is true that the relationship of a suffering or sinful person to Christ crucified may have been overly sentimentalized in the past, at least for contemporary taste. Examples of this can be found in certain forms of the stations of the cross, devotions to the five wounds, and in the chorales and other non-biblical material incorporated into even the great musical settings of the passions by Bach and others. The insight, however, that each person is invited to personal communion and identification with Christ is solid and needs to be explored and deepened with the person as the sacraments are celebrated.

Communion and identification with Christ

The last words of Christ, for example, identify his own passage. They can be read and felt by a suffering person going through various experiences and stages while coming to terms with the reality of mortality.

The gospels depict Jesus as embracing, in his passion, the deeply human experiences of emptiness, frustration and isolation—even the sense that God is distant and uncaring. The cry, "My God, my God, why have you forsaken me?"expresses these dark feelings (Matthew 27:45 and Mark 15:34).

Likewise the gospels recognize that there is an agenda to attend to and unfinished business to complete. "Father, forgive them. They do not know what they are doing" (Luke 24:34). "Truly, I tell you, today you will be with me in paradise" (Luke 24:43). "Woman, here is your son. Son, here is your mother" (John 19:26-27). "I am thirsty" (John 19:28). The business of Jesus on the cross is not unlike that of other persons experiencing, not only imminent death, but also serious illness. It is the business of reconciling, reassuring, assuring the future of those closest to him and longing that his life dream come to fulfilment.

Finally there comes the sense of closure or completeness when he cries out, "Father, into your hands I commend my spirit" (Luke 24:46), or "It is finished" (John 19:30), or even that last gesture in the fourth gospel where Jesus "bowed his head and gave up his spirit" (John 19:30).

The last moments of Jesus indicate more than a mere quiet resignation: this is a real passage. Jesus actively gives himself in absolute trust. The gospels give every indication that in these moments, even before the resurrection, his glory is being revealed.

The Christian person, baptized into the mystery of the dead and risen Christ, is invited to experience, first, the passage from strength, power, and productiveness to weakness, dependency, and helplessness. Only then can the Christian pass to "fullness of life"—whether in this world or the world to come. Christians experience this passage through, with and in Christ. The Christian lives, works, suffers and dies in solidarity with and in communion with Christ. Perhaps the Letter to the Hebrews, which expresses this truth in the most clearly "ritual" or "liturgical" language, can help establish a link with the high priesthood of Christ's "non-liturgical" self-sacrifice:

> Every high priest chosen from among mortals is put in charge of things pertaining to God on their behalf, to offer gifts and sacrifices for sins. He is able to deal gently with the ignorant and wayward, since he himself is subject to weakness; and because of this he must offer sacrifice for his own sins as well as for those of the people. And one does not presume to take this honour, but takes it only when called by God, just as Aaron was.

> So also Christ did not glorify himself in becoming a high priest, but was appointed by the one who said to him, "You are my Son, today I have begotten you"; and as he says in another place, "You are a priest forever, according to the order of Melchizedek."

> In the days of his flesh, Jesus offered up prayers and supplications, with loud cries and tears, to the one who was able to save him from death, and he was heard because of his reverent submission. Although he was a Son, he learned obedience through what he suffered; and having been made perfect, he became the source of eternal salvation for all who obey him, having been designated by God a high priest according to the order of Melchizedek (Hebrews 5:1-10).

An individual Christian's call to the cross can be celebrated, because sickness and other forms of human weakness and vulnerability are celebrated in the holy mysteries.

Renewal of baptismal anointing

A hint, however oblique, of how this takes place can be found in what is perhaps the most significant early reference to the blessing of oil. It points out the intimate relationship between the significance of oil used in initiation and in healing. Consecrations for mission, holiness and health can all be identified in the prayer found in *The Apostolic Tradition*, of Hippolytus, dating from around 215:

> If anyone offers oil, (the bishop) shall render thanks in the same way as for the offering of bread and wine, not saying (it) word for word but with similar effect, saying:
>
> O God, sanctifier of this oil, as you give health to [Dix renders the word "sanctify"] those who use and receive that with which you anointed kings, priests, and prophets, so may it give strength to all those who taste it and health to all who use it.[12]

In discussing the sacrament, Thomas Talley draws out these relationships more fully and explicitly:

> The object of the rite of anointing can be understood as renewal of the baptismal anointing by which each of us is *Christos* so that the suffering and separation of sickness become identified as participation in the *Pascha Christi*. By such anointing *anamnesis* is made of the passage of Christ through death to life and of the patient's consecration to that mystery. By such anointing, further, the suffering of the illness is oriented to a reopened future, a sense of movement in Christ through the present passion toward the kingdom.

Sickness becomes a work, a work of learning in act that for those who are his, there is no suffering that is not his. Thus the separation and humiliation of suffering becomes invitation to a *conversio* from which one never returns to his "former health"—the most regrettable phrase in the liturgies of anointing—but always moves into a deeper realization of life in the resurrection.[13]

In light of this "liturgical spirituality of consecration—of celebration," two central moments from within the complexus of prayers, actions and rites deserve to be highlighted in their stark but wonderfully evocative simplicity.

A. In the presence of the gathered community, after readings from the word of God, the priest, ideally the pastor, imposes hands upon the person in silence. This sign evokes the depths of sacramentality: a communication of the Spirit, the embrace of the community, physical connection with the great tradition of the church's compassion and solidarity with the needy. The community is "in touch."

As he anoints the person's head and hands he says:

Through this holy anointing, may the Lord in his love and mercy help you with the grace of the Holy Spirit. May the Lord who frees you from sin save you and raise you up.

After each invocation, the community, of which the sick person is a member, responds "Amen."

B. When death is near, the sick person and all present share communion under both forms. Note that the minister of communion is not necessarily ordained.

Minister: This is the bread of life.

Taste and see that the Lord is good.

All: Lord, I am not worthy to receive you,
    but, only say the word and I shall be healed.

Minister: The body of Christ.
    The dying person: Amen.

Minister: The blood of Christ.
    The dying person: Amen.

After giving communion to the dying person, the minister adds: May the Lord Jesus protect you and lead you to eternal life.

Others present who wish to share in communion do so in the usual way.

A period of silence is kept.[14]

The rites accompanying the sick and the dying celebrate Christian hope. This hope is not founded on the limits of human imagination or limited by the unadventurous paths that we humans are inclined to map out for ourselves. It is founded rather on the power and love of the living God.[15]

The liturgy has a wonderful eloquence in this regard. For Christians, it is the most powerful word and sign with which to mark such profound moments of faith. The "Amen" of the liturgy always has the last word. It is the ultimate response of persons and communities to the mysterious unfolding of their covenant with God—in good times and in bad. The "Amen" in the rites for the sick and the dying is a final word of peace. It is not a reluctant or grudging acceptance of what is unavoidable, but a believing and loving welcome of the risen Christ who embodies our absolute future.[16]

Notes

1.   Paul VI, *Apostolic Constitution, Sacrament of the Anointing of the Sick,* November 30, 1972. Published in *Pastoral Care* (Ottawa: Canadian Conference of Catholic Bishops, 1983), pp. 5-9.

2.   Congregation for Divine Worship, *General Introduction to the Rites of Anointing and Viaticum.* Published in *Pastoral Care* (Ottawa: Canadian Conference of Catholic Bishops, 1983), pp. 10-22.

3.   Congregation for Divine Worship, Prot. no. 1501/72, Published in *Pastoral Care.*

4.   Prot. no. 1501/72 describes the elements of pastoral care and invites various configurations of these elements: "The Church shows this solicitude, not only by visiting those who are in poor health but also by raising them up through the sacrament of anointing and by nourishing them with the eucharist during their illness and when they are in danger of death. Finally, the Church offers prayers for the sick to commend them to God, especially in the last crisis of life.

    "To make the meaning of the sacrament of anointing clearer and more evident, Vatican Council II decreed: 'The number of the anointings is to be adapted to the circumstances; the prayers that belong to the rite of anointing are to be so revised that they correspond to the varying conditions of the sick who receive the sacrament.' The Council also directed that a continuous rite be prepared according to which the sick person is anointed after the sacrament of penance and before receiving viaticum."

5.   The *General Introduction* also notes: "Although closely linked with the human condition, sickness cannot as a general rule be regarded as a punishment inflicted on each individual for personal sins (see John 9:3). Christ himself, who is without sin, in fulfilling the words of Isaiah took on all the wounds of his passion and shared in all human pain (see Isaiah 53:4-5). Christ is still pained and tormented in his members, made like him. Still, our afflictions seem but momentary and slight when compared to the greatness of the eternal glory for which they prepare us (see 2 Corinthians 4:17)."

6.   The centrality of the sick person, who, in a sense, becomes a "sacrament" of God's presence and action in Christ, is well expressed in David N. Power, "Let the Sick Man Call," *The Heythrop Journal* 19 (1978), p. 256/270.

7.   Joseph Pieper, *In Tune with the World, A Theory of Festivity* (New York: Harcourt Brace, and World, 1965), 81 pp. In this slim volume Pieper describes festivity in terms of the celebration of

life itself under various symbols and points to the potential impoverishment of the world without meaningful ritual.

8.   Pieper notes: "Underlying all festive joy kindled by a specific circumstance there has to be an absolutely universal affirmation extending to the world as a whole, to the reality of things and the existence of man himself. Naturally, this approval need not be a product of conscious reflection; it need not be formulated at all. Nevertheless, it remains the sole foundation for festivity, no matter what happens to be celebrated *in concreto*. And as the radical nature of negation deepens, and consequently as anything but ultimate arguments becomes ineffectual, it becomes more necessary to refer to this ultimate foundation. By ultimate foundation I mean the conviction that the prime festive occasion, which alone can ultimately justify all celebration, really exists; that, to reduce it to the most concise phrase, at bottom *everything that is, is good, and it is good to exist.* For [hu]man[s] cannot have the experience of receiving what is loved, unless the world and existence as a whole represent something good and therefore beloved to him[them].

   "Need we bother to say how little such affirmation has to do with shallow optimism, let alone with smug approval of that which is? Such affirmation is not won by deliberately shutting one's eyes to the horrors in this world. Rather, it proves its seriousness by its confrontation with historical evil. The quality of this assent is such that we must attribute it even to martyrs, at the very moment, perhaps, that they perish under brutal assault . . . whoever refuses assent to reality as a whole, no matter how well off he may be, is by that fact incapacitated for either joy or festivity."

9.   Bernard Cooke in *Sacraments and Sacramentality* (Mystic, CN: Twenty Third Publications, 1983) devotes Chapter VII (pp. 79-94) to "Christian Marriage as Basic Sacrament." He discusses it even before initiation sacraments as the lived sign of God's way of being in covenant.

10.   Peter Berger, *A Rumour of Angels,* (Garden City, NY, Doubleday, 1969), p. 67.

11.   Rabbi Harold Kushner, *Who Needs God* (New York: Summit Books, 1989), page 27.

12.   Geoffrey J. Cuming, *Hippolytus: a Text for Students* (Bramcote Notts: Grove Books, 1976), page 11.

13.   Thomas Talley, "Healing: Sacrament or Charism," in Michael Taylor, S.J., ed., *The Sacraments: Readings in Contemporary Sacramental Theology* (New York: Alba House,

1981), p. 248. It should be noted that "return to former health" to which he refers is not found in the rite currently in use in the Roman Catholic tradition.

14.   Two valuable general resources for further study are: James L. Empereur, S.J., *Prophetic Anointing* (Wilmington: Glazier, 1982), 275 pp., and Robert L. Kinast, *Sacramental Pastoral Care* (New York: Pueblo, 1988), 265 pp.

15.   *Life and Sacrament, Reflections on the Catholic Vision* by Bishop Donald Murray (Wilmington: Glazier, 1983), 135 pp., provides an excellent pastoral approach to what the author calls the deep amazement at human worth, dignity and potential inspired by the content of liturgical celebrations. Chapter 5 on suffering is particularly relevant to these reflections.

16.   See Empereur and Kinast, note 14.

Liturgy, justice and the formation of bishops

J. Frank Henderson

On several occasions I have heard Archbishop James Hayes tell the following story, which pokes gentle fun at himself and other bishops. He tells it with twinkling eyes, wide smile and hearty laughter. The story is couched in terms of an interest Roman Catholics sometimes have had in "the sacramental moment"—exactly when sacraments are thought to "happen":

> Someone who had witnessed the ordination of a bishop asked, "When exactly did it happen? At what point in the liturgy did the kind, gentle, pious and loving young presbyter whom we knew and respected become that old so-and-so of a bishop?"

This story, based on a sacramental theology that has now been superseded, assumes a more negative image of bishops than anyone would seriously entertain. The basic questions embedded in this story, nevertheless, are pertinent and profound: how and when do persons become bishops; what are the predominant characteristics of the episcopal life and ministry?

Certain members of the church begin to be bishops in the liturgy of episcopal ordination. Becoming bishops, however, is also a lifelong task that is never entirely completed. How then do newly ordained bishops learn how to become bishops more and more fully as they live the episcopal life? How are they formed in the episcopal ministry year after year?

New bishops have the example of bishops that came before them, as well as that of bishops with whom they served as presbyters; they have the advice and counsel of their contemporaries in the episcopal college; they have canon law and the decisions of other church authorities; they have the documents of Vatican Council II, especially the *Constitution on the Church* and the *Decree on the Bishops' Pastoral Office in the Church.*

More important than these, however, are the liturgies in which bishops participate, especially when they preside. The liturgy of the church, for bishops as for other Christians, is the "first teacher." Among other things, the liturgy teaches what it means to be bishops. Regular participation in the liturgy forms all of us in our Christian lives; it forms bishops in the episcopal life.

One aspect of Christian life that liturgy teaches is justice; it forms us as people who live justly.[1] My thesis is that liturgies at which bishops preside show us that justice is intrinsic to episcopal life and ministry; participation in such liturgies, at least ideally, forms bishops as persons who do justice, who live justly and who model justice in the church.

We will consider the confirmation liturgy, and the rites of installation, ordination, blessing and dedication included in the liturgical book traditionally called the pontifical.[2] Several stories from the life and ministry of Archbishop James Hayes illustrate this essay and make it more concrete.[3]

Making a commitment to justice

The liturgy of ordination of bishops—the first liturgical step in the lifelong process of becoming bishops—is explicit regarding justice. Bishops-elect are asked, "Are you resolved to show kindness and compassion in the name of the Lord to the poor and to strangers and to all who are in need?" The bishops-elect respond, "I am."

This dialogue is a pledge, the making of a commitment, the acceptance of a responsibility. It is the seventh of nine questions that comprise the "Examination of the Candidate," in which bishops-elect are asked about their "resolve to uphold the faith and to discharge [their] duties faithfully." Unless they say "I am," they cannot be ordained.

Who are the poor, strangers, and all in need to whose welfare new bishops make a commitment? "The poor" includes persons who are not well off economically, women and men who are weak and powerless and persons whose human dignity is not respected. It refers as well to persons who are unemployed or underemployed, those who do not receive just wages or appropriate fringe benefits and persons inadequately cared for by the "welfare" systems of our society.

"Strangers" includes immigrants and refugees, persons who have had to move because they have lost jobs elsewhere and persons around the world whom we may never meet or see except, perhaps, through newspapers or television. It also refers to persons who are marginalized in society, such as native peoples and persons with disabilities.

Today, unfortunately, there are "strangers" within the Christian community as well. Not a few persons feel unaccepted or unwelcome in, ignored by, or excluded from, the church: some women, children, youth, elderly women and men, persons with disabilities, aboriginal peoples, persons who have been abused—sexually, physically or emotionally—by clergy or religious, and persons whose marriage difficulties find no relief in canon law. There are also "theological strangers": other churches, other faiths and persons of no faith.

Bishops will live out their ordination pledge to do justice by getting to know personally persons who are poor, as well as strangers and all those in need. Bishops will talk with these people, listen to them and then act in concrete and visible ways to help them. Living the episcopal life will include setting personal examples of kindness and compassion as a regular and integral part of this way of life. Bishops will always act with sensitivity and respect, not in patronizing or paternalistic ways. They will affirm the dignity of persons in need; they will live and act in solidarity with strangers and the poor. The living out of their ordination commitment to do justice is integral to the lifelong process of becoming a bishop.

> *Archbishop Hayes is a staunch non-smoker, and does not want people to smoke around him. He also has an incredible sense of people in need and the human face of weakness. At his office he almost always made time to see the people living on the streets and provided them with bus tickets, grocery vouchers, money and sometimes work. At other times he would send one of his staff to a home with a bag of groceries or other basic living items. One night I got a call to go and pick up some tobacco for a man living in a nearby group home.*

This man needed to smoke, and the bishop (the non-smoker) recognized his need and still provided for him.

Archbishop Hayes' kindness always shone through and was so evident when it came to the homeless and street people. Once someone showed up at his office at lunch hour and demanded attention. The archbishop was about to enter a luncheon meeting. Instead he asked me to tell the group that he had something to attend to and would be back in time for the meeting. They were to eat without him. He left with the homeless man and took him to a restaurant for lunch.

Building churches of justice

In the liturgy of dedication of a church, the church building is an icon or metaphor for the "real" church: the baptized people of God. The prayer at the centre of this rite names "the mystery of the church" in a variety of ways. At the climax of this prayer, presiding bishops proclaim, "Here may the poor find justice, the victims of oppression, true freedom." Through the anointings that follow, these characteristics of the church are symbolically written on the altar and on the walls of the church building, hence also on the hearts and hands of the people who comprise the church.

There are far too many "victims of oppression" in our world today. Many experience political, economic, intellectual, sexual, physical, psychological and other forms of oppression. Sadly, oppression sometimes occurs in the church as well.

The formation of bishops as persons who do justice progresses each time they celebrate the liturgy of dedication. This process is deepened when bishops celebrate any liturgy in churches dedicated to justice and true freedom. These liturgical "rehearsals" prepare bishops to ensure that the church communities in which they preside are also places of justice and true freedom for the poor and victims of oppression.

"True freedom" is the potential to be who one is called to be; it is the ability to live life to its fullness. To find justice and true freedom means that poor persons and victims of oppression will actually experience these qualities of life. This goes beyond simply wishing and praying for them.

Justice and true freedom need to be experienced in the liturgies celebrated in church buildings whose walls and altar are anointed with these gospel words. Liturgies that are just and in which true freedom is experienced are inclusive; they include and unite persons in the local community, persons all around the world, and ourselves and all of creation.

Liturgies that are experiences of justice and true freedom empower women and men and give them life. They enable people to be who God calls them to be; remember the ancient saying, "The glory of God is the human person fully alive." Liturgies that are just raise up God's dream for humanity and all of creation: the reign of God. They illumine a God that is bigger than our imagining. They open our eyes to new ways of seeing and dreaming, so that we may share God's dream and live accordingly. The regular celebration of such liturgies is an important part of the lifelong formation of bishops in their ministry of justice.

Bishops and all members of the church are then called to live out the implications of such liturgical celebrations in all aspects of church life as well as in our civic, national and worldwide communities. As leaders of local church communities, bishops need to show that the words "here may the poor find justice, the victims of oppression, true freedom" are indeed written on their hearts and hands.

> One day we were gathered for a buffet lunch. Archbishop Hayes arrived after everyone else and filled a plate to overflowing. He then disappeared. He returned a few minutes later, prepared another plate and sat down to eat with us. Later, we discovered he had taken the food to a hungry man who had stopped him as he came in.

> Archbishop Hayes has always made it a point to ensure that children with mental handicaps were carefully prepared to celebrate the sacraments.

Praying for the transforming Spirit

A number of episcopal liturgies include prayers of consecration that invoke the transforming presence of the Holy Spirit. Thus bishops lead assemblies in praying, "Send your Holy Spirit upon them to be their Helper and Guide" (confirmation); "Lord, send forth upon him the Holy Spirit" (ordination of deacons); "Renew within him the Spirit of holiness" (ordination of presbyters); "So now pour out upon this chosen one that power which is from you, the governing Spirit" (ordination of bishops); "Give [him/her] the gifts of your Spirit (blessings of abbots and of abbesses); "Through the gift of your Spirit, Lord, give them..." (consecration of virgins); "Lord, send your Spirit from heaven" (dedication of a church); "...send the Holy Spirit" (blessing of the oil of the sick); and "Fill it with the power of your Holy Spirit" (consecration of chrism).

In these texts liturgical assemblies pray to God to send the Holy Spirit. By tradition such prayers are voiced by their bishop presiders, but they are not prayers of the bishops alone, isolated from the rest of the local church. Likewise, the Holy Spirit is always God's gift, not the personal gift of the bishop presiders.

The Spirit that God sends is the Spirit of justice, the Spirit of sanctification, consecration, conversion and transformation. The presence of the Spirit brings about new ways of being, new ways of living; in plain language, the Spirit brings about change. When we ask God to send the Holy Spirit, we are asking for the power to change. The doing of justice and the living of just lives requires and implies change—transformation, conversion. They also require the strength, vision and empowerment that are the Holy Spirit's gifts.

Each time bishops invoke the Holy Spirit in the liturgy, the process of their formation as ministers of justice continues. Bishops will be receptive to change and agents of change inasmuch as they lead prayers for God's transforming gift of the Holy Spirit. And transformation for the sake of justice, not the maintenance of the status quo, expresses the authentic tradition.

The formation of bishops as justice ministers responsive to the empowering breath of the Spirit brings flexibility and openness to surprises. Transformation, by its very nature, cannot be completely predicted and, although spirits do need to be discerned, bishops also need to be open to the unexpected in the Spirit's activities. The journey of pilgrim people, whether Israel, the early church or the church today, could not and cannot be completely charted ahead of time.

One year we were without a pastor at Easter. On Holy Thursday I drove to the city for the Chrism Mass, then went back home to prepare our church for the evening mass. Not wanting to leave us without the celebrations of the triduum, Archbishop Hayes came to preside for us. I was conscious that he had had a very long day and must be tired. I know I was! Following mass, I was preparing to spend some time in prayer during the hours before midnight. The bishop came into the church and I remember thinking that now he could rest in prayer, too. Instead he came over and said, "Are there any sick among you? Will you take me out to visit at the hospital now, please?" He could not rest until he had cared for those who could not be with us at eucharist that night.

Engaging in dialogues of peace

The core of the liturgy of confirmation concludes with a dialogue in which bishop presiders say, "Peace be with you," and the newly confirmed woman or man responds, "And also with you." In other liturgies the same dialogue is exchanged between bishop presiders and the liturgical assembly as a whole; by tradition, presbyters do not use this particular greeting.

The sign or kiss of peace includes the same dialogue together with some gesture of peace. This sign is part of many episcopal liturgies: ordinations of deacons, presbyters and bishops; blessings of abbots and of abbesses; the consecration of virgins.

"Peace be with you" / "And also with you" is a dialogue. Both persons speak; both listen. It is an exchange of speech between two persons who are paying attention to each other. In some liturgies both may also touch each other in some way.

To engage in dialogues of peace is to do justice and to experience justice. Every time these dialogues occur in the liturgy, bishop presiders and people alike are being formed as women and men of justice.

Dialogues of peace are experiences of mutuality in which both partners show their respect and care for each other; they pray for one another, they try to really communicate with one another. Each has to listen; each needs to hear the other; each needs to accept the speech and prayer that is communicated to them. This dialogue should never degenerate into mere formality or empty words. The one who speaks first needs to wait for the response and receive it as a precious gift.

The liturgical dialogue of peace—and the many other liturgical dialogues—shows bishops that dialogue is the most appropriate mode of communication among persons. The regular liturgical experience of engaging in dialogue helps to form bishops to do justice in the way they communicate with individuals, local church communities and the wider society.

> A few years ago Archbishop Hayes agreed to preside at eucharist and preach at the Archdiocesan Youth Festival. Before the festival began he asked about the theme, the workshops and other activities about the festival to gain some insight into what would be happening there. It was obvious when he preached that he had done his homework. He guided the young people by focusing on the gospel and then began to bring that message to the present, to their lives today. He began to ask the young people what was important to them. He then began to quote the brand names of jeans, shirts, shoes and music that the young people find important and meaningful. By using language and images that they understood he was able to connect their experience and the gospel.

Peace is a characteristic and goal of doing justice and of living justly; peace cannot be accomplished without justice. Liturgical celebration will form bishops to be ministers committed to peace in all their personal relationships and dealings with people. Every kind of violence—whatever is not peace—will be eschewed, including every kind of misuse of ecclesiastical power.

Bishops will actively promote, seek and bring peace wherever it is absent: in situations of ethnic violence, terrorism and war; of violence against women and children, of the violence of political and economic powers. Bishops will seek to bring peace within the church as well. Conflict between persons of differing theological views and differing visions of church needs to be diminished, not by suppression, but by increasing mutual understanding. Conflicts between church employees or volunteers and pastors or supervisors need to be brought to resolution. Conflicts in ecumenical and interfaith relations need to be encompassed in the dialogue of peace as well.

To be formed as peace-maker through liturgical and pastoral ministry is to live in the peace or *shalom* of scripture; peace is another name for the reign of God.

Touching with gentleness

Presiding bishops gently lay hands on the heads of their sisters and brothers in the liturgy of confirmation and the liturgies of ordination of deacons, presbyters and bishops. Most will also be gently touched again in the anointing with chrism that is part of all of these liturgies except the ordination of deacons. (The days of bishops slapping children on the cheek at confirmation are over, thank God!)

The laying on of hands is a gentle touch. Anointing with chrism adorns persons with something beautiful. Both these gestures are embraces or caresses.

Physical touching is a symbol for any kind of contact or relationship between persons. Relating to others in a spirit of gentleness is a form of doing justice, a manifestation of just living. Bishops learn gentle relationships from the liturgy. This practice forms them as persons of justice for all situations in which they touch or relate to others. In a world that surrounds us with so much physical and verbal violence, bishops will model gentleness in relationships among people.

> One day I pulled into the Pastoral Centre parking lot just in time to see Archbishop Hayes get into this very old, very rickety, souped-up car with two dangerous-looking characters. They were unshaven, unwashed, and, to my eyes, rather frightening. I was afraid for the bishop. A short time later the car came back; the bishop got out and waved as the men drove away. It turned out they were trying to get home to a distant village for a family funeral, and had run out of money. Archbishop Hayes had taken them to get a tank of gas and a little food. He had no concern for his safety.

Anointing with chrism does not so much make someone beautiful as affirm each person's fundamental beauty, dignity and worth. Such affirmation is greatly needed today; to affirm others is part of the ministry of justice. The liturgical experience of affirming people will form bishops as leaders in affirming the enormous beauty, dignity and worth of every human person.

Giving away gifts for service

In the course of the various installations, ordinations and blessings of persons at which bishops preside, they give away gifts that are used in ministry and in the Christian lives of the individuals concerned. Bibles are given to readers; books of the gospels to deacons and bishops; vessels with bread or wine to acolytes; rings to bishops, abbots, abbesses and virgins; pastoral staffs to bishops and abbots; religious rules to abbots, abbesses and virgins who are members of religious congregations; miters to bishops and abbots; stoles to deacons and presbyters; dalmatics to deacons; chasubles to presbyters; and veils to virgins.

The central words of the liturgy of confirmation undergird these kinds of gift-giving: "N., be sealed with the Gift of the Holy Spirit." All members of the church receive this gift; some members also receive the more concrete and material gifts mentioned above. Some of these gifts may be considered "tools" for ministry; others are symbols of a particular ministry or way of living the Christian life. In all cases God is the real gift-giver; bishops are faithful servants.

Giving things to others is one dimension of doing justice; giving gifts—of all kinds—is part of living justly. What bishops practise in the liturgy forms them as "givers" in all aspects of their episcopal life and ministry. Bishops will delight, therefore, in giving away gifts of all kinds that will bring life to Christian people or will facilitate Christian ministries of all sorts.

To be a minister of God's gift-giving will make bishops aware that every thing and every person is gift. If such is the case, then clinging to possessions or power, as well as trying to limit or manipulate God's gifts, is out of the question. In and out of the liturgy, generous giving and thankful living are the only appropriate responses to God's generosity. Part of the lifelong formation of bishops, therefore, includes the practice and attitude of generosity in giving.

> *One day a man called, saying that he was in hospital and needed clothes to wear before he would be released. Archbishop Hayes left the meeting, drove to Dartmouth (a considerable distance on a bitterly cold day), and brought shoes and other items of his own clothing so that the man could leave the hospital.*

Ministering face to face

Most of the liturgies at which bishops preside recognize or involve individual members of the church in some special way; in almost every case there is one-to-one interaction between bishop presiders and individual participants. Bishops recognize each as an individual person; they say, at least implicitly, "You are church; you are sister or brother; you are friend in Jesus Christ and the Spirit."

To recognize and respect others as individual persons is part of living justly. The liturgical experience of ministering face to face will help to form bishops in their episcopal life and ministry. Bishops need always to relate to members of their diocesan church as individuals, as sisters and brothers, as friends, in all their ministry and in their daily lives. To become impersonal, remote, bureaucratic, out of touch or office-bound is inconsistent with this dimension of their liturgical formation as persons of justice.

Archbishop Rembert G. Weakland of Milwaukee has recently spoken of the gulf that he discerns in the United States between the church hierarchy and the laity.[4] According to the press account, "few lay people see the U. S. Catholic bishops 'as understanding where they are coming from, as forming a part of their daily struggles, or as examples of Christian living to be imitated.'" The story continues:

> Weakland said he senses that lay Catholics today "do not want to be treated as children but as adults, not as idiots but as responsible and conscientious followers of Christ. They want a hierarchy that listens more, is a part of their common struggle and does not give the pretension of having the answer before the question is even formulated," he added. "They want bishops who share their lives more directly and do not stand above them or outside their daily quandaries. They want leaders who believe that the Holy Spirit is in the whole People of God and not just in themselves."

This analysis implies that the liturgical experience of ministering face to face has not been applied in some bishops' pastoral ministry, at least in ways that are experienced by the lay people to whom Archbishop Weakland refers.

> *So many people tell of the archbishop coming to spend long hours praying at the bedside of one who was dying. He knew it was the most important thing he could do.*

> *Each year a team is gathered to plan and implement our Youth Festival. The social aspect of the team formation is as important as the other dimensions of leadership. One year the team decided that all team members would wear a Hawaiian shirt to help identify them. As with other decisions, this was recorded in the minutes. When Archbishop Hayes dropped by to visit with some of the young people at the festival, he arrived with a grin on his face and surprised all of us by*

wearing a beautiful pale blue Hawaiian shirt. With open mouths and smiling faces the team knew right away that he had taken the time to read the minutes and that he was with them.

Living as chief liturgist

Bishops are sometimes called the "chief liturgists" of their diocesan churches. This does not mean the chief rubricists, or the chief enforcers of liturgical rules and regulations or the chief arbiters of "liturgical correctness." To be chief liturgists is to enter especially deeply into the liturgy and to express its meaning and consequences in living daily as persons of justice. As chief liturgists, bishops will embrace their formation in the episcopal life and ministry that the liturgies of the church provide. They will see, appreciate and live out the ministry of justice that is at the centre of all liturgical celebrations.

Liturgy, justice and the formation of bishops

Liturgies in which bishops preside show us that justice is intrinsic to episcopal life and ministry. Participation in such liturgies provides bishops with opportunities to be formed as persons who do justice, who live justly, and who model justice in the church. Let those who have eyes to see. . . .

Notes

1.   See, for example, J. Frank Henderson, Stephen Larson and Kathleen Quinn, *Liturgy, Justice, and the Reign of God: Vision and Practice* (New York: Paulist, 1987); J. Frank Henderson and Kathleen Quinn, "Justice, Injustice and Sunday Worship," *National Bulletin on Liturgy*, vol. 26, no. 135 (Winter, 1993), pp. 214-23; Kathleen Quinn and J. Frank Henderson, "Liturgy, Justice, and Daily Life," *National Bulletin on Liturgy*, vol. 26, no. 135 (Winter, 1993), pp. 224-32.

2.   Volume Two of *The Rites of the Catholic Church as Revised by Decree of the Second Vatican Ecumenical Council and Published by Authority of Pope Paul VI* (New York: Pueblo Publishing Co., 1980).

3.   In their modesty the co-workers of Archbishop Hayes who recounted these stories did not wish their names acknowledged here.

4.   "Great gulf between bishops and people: Weakland," *Prairie Messenger*, December 13, 1993, p. 5.

Learning a "new" eucharistic language

William Marrevee, S.C.J.

Learning to work effectively with a system of measurement different from the one with which you have grown up can be an unsettling experience. Is it just by chance that the changeover from the imperial system to the metric was called "conversion"? It takes effort to use litres, metres and kilograms with ease. Particularly revealing is that when, in the initial phases of familiarization with the new system, we encounter an unexpected, new situation, we tend to revert spontaneously to the former, more familiar system. We need a more relaxed setting to handle the new situation with our newly acquired skills.

This situation exhibits a striking similarity to the experience of many faith communities—I am thinking of otherwise viable parishes in particular—that want to continue assembling for worship on Sunday, but must do so without a presbyter. Initially, to cope with this relatively new situation, many parishes resort to "communion services." After a liturgy of the word, they take communion using hosts consecrated at a previous eucharist. This practice is a good example of how, when faced with a critical situation, we turn to tools with which we have grown up. We lack the necessary confidence to apply our newly acquired tools.

In this essay I would like to argue that having recourse to communion services on Sunday in the circumstances described is a consequence of the eucharistic language that we, as Catholics, have spoken with great ease for a good number of centuries. Faced with not having a priest to preside at the community's Sunday eucharist, we are reluctant to or lack the confidence to speak, with some degree of consistency, the eucharistic language emerging as a result of the attempted eucharistic reform of this century. So we revert to the eucharistic language that has been standard for many centuries. Because we are not conversant enough with the language this century's eucharistic reform offers us, we cannot use it to help us meet the challenge of this new situation.

Is the difference between the two eucharistic languages so great that one would more easily allow for communion services while the other would raise serious objections to it? While it is dangerous to simplify, there is a marked difference.

The eucharistic language we have spoken for so long is marked by the eucharistic controversies of the eleventh and the sixteenth centuries. It is also a language that has compartmentalized a number of aspects of the one eucharist. The eucharistic language we are trying to speak as part of this century's eucharistic reform avoids controversies and is more biblically and liturgically rooted and, thus, more traditional. It better protects the unity and inner coherence of the various aspects of the eucharist.

The eucharistic language shaped by controversies

It is far beyond the scope of this essay to deal in detail with the various factors that led to the eleventh and the sixteenth centuries' controversies or to the actual shape of these controversies. Yet, they are at the heart of the eucharistic language that has prevailed for so long. The eleventh-century controversy centred around the issue of what has come to be known as the real presence of Christ in the consecrated species of bread and wine. The resolution of the issue gave rise to a more object-oriented preoccupation and a more prominent position of the priest. These two factors effectively replaced the understanding of eucharist as a set of interdependent actions of the celebrating community. Although this controversy will flare up again in the sixteenth century, albeit in a slightly different form and in connection with other concerns, the basic shape of the issue and the language that accompanies it are pretty much established in the earlier part of the second millennium.

The sixteenth-century controversy on the sacrifice of the mass is of a considerably different make-up. It is an integral part of the even more substantive and more inclusive controversy with the reformers that resulted in the breakup of the church in the west. Subtle shifts in the notion of priesthood had occasioned and strengthened the emergence of the sacrifice of the mass as an issue. A sacrificing notion of priesthood had become prominent, virtually replacing the ministry of presiding over the eucharistic community. The monopoly, in the west, of the Roman canon, in which the terminology of sacrifice and offering crowds out almost every other aspect inherent to a eucharistic prayer, also played an important role in shaping the eucharistic language. Whatever its merits, the emphasis on the sacrificial nature of the mass and the elaborate system of masses that grew up around it resulted in an unnecessary, but very powerful, narrowing of focus.

We need to pay attention to the impact of these two issues on eucharistic practice and thought, and to the shape they have given and still continue to give to our eucharistic discourse. It is particularly important to note that, as a result, the polemics surrounding the issues have drawn disproportionate attention to them. These issues, two aspects of a larger whole, in no way exhaust the mystery of the eucharist. The impression is given easily, however, that they address the entire reality of the eucharist. They easily overshadow equally important, if not more important, aspects of the eucharist. That is one of the unfortunate side effects of controversies. Legitimate aspects that are emphasized and placed under scrutiny take on such prominence that they begin to lead an almost independent existence, and tend to make exclusive claims for themselves.

The disproportionate attention given to the issues of real presence and the sacrifice of the mass also affects the practice of communion, which is of more immediate concern to us. What is the relationship between, on the one hand, the emergence of real presence and sacrifice as the all-important eucharistic issues and, on the other, the decline of sharing the consecrated bread and wine by the celebrating community? I am not suggesting there is a cause-effect relationship between them. I do believe, however, that a link exists. So much energy went into the controversies that the actual practice of taking communion was neglected, not only in practice, but also in theological reflection. The controversial issues of real presence and sacrifice were resolved with little attention given to the integral aspect of the sharing of the body and blood of Christ, leaving the impression that these issues exhausted the mystery of the eucharist, and that communion is not really integral to it. This approach sets the scene for the actual practice of taking communion independently of the eucharistic action of which it is a constitutive element. With the facility we have gained over the centuries to speak this sort of eucharistic language, it is no wonder that today we have recourse to the virtually independent communion service.

The developments we have briefly outlined were enshrined in the official teaching of the Roman Catholic Church at the Council of Trent. Characteristic of its legacy, which has been so much part of Catholic eucharistic discourse for the last four centuries, is that it deals with three aspects of the one eucharist in three separate documents: real presence (1551), communion (1562) and sacrifice (1562). There is no significant attempt at integration. The separation of these aspects became the established pattern, leaving the impression that the official declarations about these issues in the documents of Trent contained the church's entire teaching on the eucharist. Even some potentially fortunate and enriching developments in the earlier part of this century, such as more frequent communion, did not fundamentally alter the separation of the aspects mentioned. These developments themselves were simply part of the eucharistic language that has dominated the second millennium.

Characteristic of this eucharistic language is its distance from biblical sources and from the actual eucharistic liturgies. It shows little evidence of familiarity with the biblical background, especially the Jewish roots, of the eucharist. Nor did it pay much attention to the eucharistic liturgy itself as the privileged source from which to engage in theological reflection about the eucharist.

Preoccupation with such controversial issues as real presence and sacrifice had become so central that it even imposed its own constraints on the eucharistic liturgies themselves. This sort of constraint can be found even in the eucharistic prayer, the very heart of the eucharist. Speaking the words of consecration in a manner that identifies the last supper narratives in the eucharistic prayer and giving prominence to sacrificial language that virtually overshadowed the thanksgiving motif are two examples.

The kind of eucharistic language that had exclusive currency in the period reveals an even more telling dislocation, resulting from the clergy-laity split so characteristic of the church of that era. In the notional world established by the ideas of real presence and sacrifice, the priest is indispensable and the notion of priesthood identified in relation to these ideas. The priest has the power to confect the real presence and to offer the sacrifice. For these aspects of the eucharist, there is no need for lay people. They enter the eucharistic scene only to receive communion. This suggests that the practice of Sunday communion services in the absence of a priest is simply a further development of the eucharistic language of the second millennium.

A more biblically and liturgically rooted eucharistic language

Exegetical, patristic and liturgical studies in this century, quite often undertaken in an ecumenical perspective, are shaping a different eucharistic language. This development is part of re-discovering some basic aspects of the eucharist too long obscured or left unattended. This has been the debit side of the legitimate concern with real presence and sacrifice. Equally important aspects of the eucharist were neither contradicted nor rejected. They were simply not part of the eucharistic discourse. The unfortunate side effect of this neglect was that the issues of real presence and sacrifice became more controversial than was necessary. With the rediscovery of these basic aspects of eucharist, still separated churches now can speak about the eucharist with an increasing degree of consensus, to which various reports and agreed statements from official ecumenical dialogue groups give ample evidence. The best example of this advance is the section devoted to the eucharist in *Baptism, Eucharist and Ministry (BEM)*, the 1982 Lima document of the Faith and Order Commission of the World Council of Churches. This is not an isolated document, but reflects the progress all churches have made in both understanding the liturgical shape of the eucharist and doing eucharistic theology.

The centuries-long debate between the separated churches about real presence and the sacrifice of the mass has contributed nothing to their reconciliation. In fact, it was part of their estrangement. Returning to the scriptures and earlier eucharistic liturgies has made possible a growing consensus on the eucharist. In its section on the meaning of the eucharist (Eucharist, II, 2), *BEM* offers the best summary of this consensus: "Although the eucharist is essentially one complete act, it will be considered here under the following aspects: thanksgiving to the Father, memorial *[anamnesis]* of Christ, invocation of the Spirit, communion of the faithful, meal of the Kingdom."

These aspects of the eucharist lay bare the basic constitutive elements of the eucharist, that is to say, the trinitarian, ecclesial and eschatological dimensions that are hardly recognizable in the concern about real presence and sacrifice. The attention given to these aspects represents a significant shift in eucharistic discourse, with implications for eucharistic practice. Practices congenial to the eucharistic language shaped by controversy may not fare as well when we consistently apply the more biblically and liturgically rooted eucharistic language.

The issues of real presence and sacrifice, which shaped the previous eucharistic language, are quite familiar to most people. The trinitarian, ecclesial and eschatological aspects of the eucharist that belong to the new eucharistic language may not be as familiar. So it may be helpful to sketch them here.

The trinitarian aspect

As the church's pre-eminent liturgical activity, the eucharist cannot be understood apart from the Jesus Christ event. In the power of the Spirit, and by means of word and ritual, this all-important Christ-event is evoked and made present so that those participating may progressively enter into it. The eucharist is the church's memorialization of Christ's paschal mystery, the foundation of Christian identity.

But here we must avoid a narrow Christocentrism. The Christ mystery itself manifests and realizes God's salvific intentions for all humanity. Through the power of the Spirit, God continues to realize these salvific intentions in humanity's history. In the praying and proclaiming mode of the eucharistic prayer, the mystery of the eucharist best reveals the mystery of the trinity. In this central part of the eucharistic liturgy the church gives praise and thanks to God the Father, remembers the Christ mystery and invokes the Holy Spirit over the gifts of bread and wine and over the assembly.

The ecclesial aspect

In the eucharistic celebration, the risen Christ, in the power of the Spirit, gives himself to his disciples in the form of the eucharistized bread and wine. That is to say, Christ makes the disciples into his body, the church, by drawing them into his self-giving in obedience to the Father and in life-giving service to others. The eucharist makes the church. The eucharist constantly brings the church back to its foundational event, its source. The bread and wine shared are the Spirit-empowered bearers of Jesus' self-giving, on which the body of Christ is privileged to feed for its own sustenance and mission.

If a narrow Christocentrism is to be avoided, so is a narrow ecclesiocentrism. The church-building effect of the eucharist must not be made an absolute. The eucharist builds us up progressively into the body of Christ, the church, so that we may come to share in the intimate life of the trinity. The celebration of the eucharist sustains and strengthens in us the life of the trinity, in which we share by a faith sealed in baptism. This trinitarian aspect is also the basis for the love and unity that characterize the eucharistic community. This love and unity are no less than the reflection of the communion of love and life among the three persons of the blessed trinity.

The eschatological aspect

A preoccupation with what happens to the bread and wine when the words of consecration are pronounced over them, and a narrow focus on how the sacrifice of the mass relates to the sacrifice on the cross have contributed to the virtual disappearance of the eschatological aspect from our eucharistic consciousness. This is all the more surprising when we see the prominence of the eschatological vision in the so-called last supper narratives. The synoptic version evokes it using the image of the kingdom of God, while Paul, in his first letter to the Corinthians, speaks of it in terms of the Lord's coming. In both instances, the eschatological vision helps situate the church-building effect of the eucharist in its proper perspective.

Precisely because the eucharist evokes and makes present the Christ mystery, it is thoroughly eschatological. If, in the Jesus Christ event, God has engaged in re-creating us and our world, then God has laid the foundation for healing and reconciling a wounded and broken humanity in this Jesus who has died and risen. The celebration of the eucharist makes us, for a moment, anticipate and, by way of promise, cherish the heavenly banquet. If charity is indeed the primary quality of the community that celebrates the eucharist, we catch a glimpse of and receive a foretaste of that day when God will bring everything together under Christ as head.

If, in the previous eucharistic language, the issues of real presence, communion and sacrifice could be dealt with separately, such an approach is entirely impossible with the trinitarian, ecclesial and eschatological aspects. They are totally interrelated; one calls forth and depends on the other and, in their interaction, they constitute the mystery of the eucharist. Moreover, the subject that engages in the eucharistic activity is the local community, over which the ordained minister presides. This is considerably different from "having the priest say mass and the faithful attend."

There is really nothing new in these three aspects of the eucharist. In fact, they are very traditional, but they have been overshadowed and ignored because of what were considered to be other more pressing eucharistic concerns. These three aspects have resurfaced, however, as a result of allowing the biblical origins of the eucharist, and the eucharistic liturgies of the first five or six centuries to have a greater say in shaping our eucharistic language. But these same aspects are also immediately evident when we attend to the basic structure and content of the eucharistic prayer in which the church articulates its eucharistic faith with the greatest authority.

At the same time, we realize that the trinitarian, ecclesial and eschatological dimensions are not constitutive of the eucharist in any exclusive sense. They apply with equal importance to the summary of the Christian faith in the form of the creed, but they are also the most elementary components of the Christian life itself. The basic features of Christian life resemble closely these characteristics of the eucharist.

• The Christian life is trinitarian: As Christians we are privileged to share in the intimate life of the trinity. We know ourselves to be sons and daughters of God: in faith and baptism we have been grafted onto Jesus Christ. He is the vine, we are the branches; the life-giving Spirit dwells in us.

• The Christian life is ecclesial: The above elements make us the body of Christ, the church, in which we are brothers and sisters to each other. None of us is a believer alone.

• The Christian life is eschatological: All that we are as Christians still awaits its completion when Christ will come in glory and raise us to fullness of life.

If the trinitarian, ecclesial and eschatological aspects are this prominent in the eucharist, in the creed and in the Christian life, then we have all the more reason to hold to the centrality of the celebration of the eucharist in the Christian faith experience. The eucharist is not simply an aspect of the Christian life, but its very heart.

Implications for communion services

The eucharistic reform of this century is intimately linked with learning to speak a different eucharistic language, one that is not immediately conditioned and imprisoned by the eucharistic controversies of the second millennium. This different eucharistic language reflects more closely the actual eucharistic liturgy and boasts stronger biblical and patristic credentials. Learning to speak this sort of eucharistic language, even tentatively and hesitantly, is a major undertaking that leads inevitably to a different way of perceiving the role and function of the eucharist in the life of the Christian community on Sunday. It may also lead to a malaise with or a questioning of the desirability, if not the legitimacy, of some eucharistic practices that flowed quite easily from the previous eucharistic language. We should not be surprised if some of these practices clash with the "new" eucharistic language we are learning to speak.

Holding a communion service on Sunday as a substitute for celebrating the eucharist is a case in point. Taking communion apart from an actual celebration of the eucharist may be quite acceptable as part of the previous eucharistic language, which thrived on separating aspects of the eucharist that really belong together. But a eucharistic language intent on incorporating and holding together the trinitarian, ecclesial and eschatological aspects of the eucharist will also respect and protect the inner coherence of the parts that make up the liturgy of the eucharist: the presentation of the gifts, the eucharistic prayer, the breaking of the bread and the communion of the eucharistized bread and wine. Each action is integral to the overall flow of the eucharistic liturgy. Seeing one part, such as the taking of communion, lead a relatively independent existence raises questions.

What meanings will be associated with the taking of communion when this action is dissociated from its original setting, especially when this dissociation threatens to become a regular practice over a long period of time? Can this practice safeguard the integrity of the eucharist? If an otherwise viable parish community is forced to have recourse to a communion service, is it effectively entering into Christ's paschal mystery, which the celebration of the eucharist memorializes and from which the church, the body of Christ, draws its identity?

The suggestion that the bread used in the communion service was consecrated at a previous eucharist does not safeguard the link with an actual celebration of the eucharist. This argument could be used with greater facility in the previous eucharistic language. But even in that language, consecrating bread at one eucharist to enable the community to have a communion service on the next few Sundays is a considerable novelty. That eucharistic language would more easily allow for this practice inasmuch as the language of real presence and sacrifice showed very little appreciation for the integrity and basic flow of the eucharistic prayer in the overall context of the eucharistic liturgy. On the other hand, a eucharistic language that originates from the integrity, both of the eucharistic prayer and the entire eucharistic action, will be at a loss to know what meaning to attribute to a communion service.

Is there not the danger that a variety of meanings will be attributed to the communion services, some of which may be difficult to reconcile with the original intent of sharing the eucharistized bread and wine in the celebration of the eucharist? A parallel development comes to mind. Once we allowed confirmation to be dissociated from baptism, it came to mean a number of things. Will taking communion as an isolated act of a community meet with the same fate? Conversely, if a community experiences communion services over a longer period of time, it is not unthinkable that it may become very difficult to re-integrate the taking of communion into a celebration of the eucharist again. After all, some people would say they have not missed very much. The only thing missing would have been the eucharistic prayer, a part of the mass that, in the previous eucharistic language, did not concern the people.

If this approach became part of the justification for communion services, then much of the eucharistic reform of this century will have gone to waste. We will have allowed the liturgical action, which has pride of place in shaping a priestly people, to disintegrate. Surely, both the treasure of the eucharist and the priestly people deserve better.

Ministry of leadership for households of faith

Mary M. Schaefer

T he rugged coastal landscape of eastern Canada's Atlantic provinces cradles picturesque villages framing irregular harbours, isolated outports, inland towns and family farms. More ubiquitous than the lighthouse, these communities are marked by one or more steepled churches. Culture, geography and demography foster both independence and collaboration among the scattered population. Religious commitment and conservatism live as easy neighbours alongside ecumenical openness and respect.

The person-to-person contact on which the ministry of the church relies is especially precious in this environment. Despite high church allegiance, not every community of some size can hope to have a resident presbyter to minister to its pastoral needs, preach the gospel, celebrate eucharist and the other sacraments, comfort the grieving and bury the dead. The Atlantic provinces face the realities long since experienced in the Canadian west and north and known at first hand by sixty-five per cent of the Roman Catholic world. Central and South America and large parts of Africa and Asia have met the problem of too few priests with itinerant ordained ministers and local lay leaders. Since their evangelization, some regions have lacked Sunday eucharistic assembly for substantial portions of the Christian year.[1]

I. The problem: shortage of eucharistic leaders

The ecclesial re-orientation required to provide sufficient leaders qualified to preside at eucharistic celebrations involves what people of the Atlantic provinces call "a sea-change": an unexpected or notable transformation of theology. Meanwhile the common or universal priesthood and the ministries of the baptized are being reclaimed. Sacramentally privileged North Americans, however, await with dismay Roman Catholic life without its central expression, regular eucharist.

In the new world mission fields, itinerant pastors and infrequent celebration of mass were once necessities. The community had brought habits of eucharistic abstinence from the old countries; the faithful attended and the priest communicated vicariously for them. Late medieval custom shaped by the Fourth Lateran Council (1215) had established as normative one communion annually at Eastertide, required under pain of mortal sin. Much Protestant practice marked a fourfold improvement in frequency of congregational communion. Roman Catholics did not, in the main, overcome their habits of eucharistic reticence until Vatican II.

For the Atlantic provinces, probable consequences of regular reliance on non-eucharistic Sunday assemblies in parishes that are "traditional" in their observance but without a full-time ordained pastor are predictable: decreased liturgical participation; reduction in the frequency of communion; reduced religious practice; a somewhat increased percentage of persons leaving the church even while the numbers of baptized rise.[2] Ironically, Catholics face this future at a time when other Christian churches are renewing biblical preaching through use of the adapted Roman lectionary, introducing liturgies inspired by the whole tradition and approaching the table with greater frequency.

Ritual behaviour is repetitive. Office-holders in communities habituated to ritual expression understandably are biased towards retaining past organizational and recruitment policies. This suggests one reason why creative response on the part of church leadership at the highest levels has been lacking so far.

Yet the community called together by God is not organized for the benefit of its office-holders. Persons hold ecclesial office because their service is deemed essential to the church's upbuilding and outpouring of itself in witness, service and worship. The ritual action that these leaders animate situates persons-in-community in a present of deepened insight and celebration grounded on the primordial sacrament, Jesus Christ, and his saving work in history. From this stance the community aspires towards God's future from whence comes Christ its Lord to meet his bride, the church.

This contribution to a volume in honour of a leader of the church in Atlantic Canada outlines a theological way forward for ministry in the twenty-first century, which must also be concerned with ecumenical bridge-building in the post-Christian global village. Elements of this proposal are recoverable from secondary traditions of the early city-church of Rome and its sister-churches of the first millennium's undivided communion of churches.

II. Why the church needs priests: every parish is eucharistic

"... a truly living community cannot resign itself to being without a priest to offer the eucharist for them...." John Paul II reminds North Americans, in the persons of bishops from several Appalachian states, of the "utterly irreplaceable" role of the priest. Sunday celebrations in the absence of a priest "offer only a temporary solution," he declares.[3] The pope's position on the centrality of eucharist to the faith community is fundamentally that articulated in the well-known Concilium volume, *The Right of the Community to a Priest*.[4] What differs is the means to a solution. John Paul hopes that prayer will reverse the ever decreasing number of active priests, and declares that Catholic theology cannot see the elimination of priests as "a providential sign that lay persons are to replace priests."[5] Reception of alternative proposals to provide communities with qualified eucharistic leaders—the ordination to priesthood of married men and of women, lay presidents of eucharist, or part-time and limited-time priests—would appear to be precluded by different operative theologies.

Signs of the times in contemporary society include the value placed on persons-in-relationship through social interchange and human sexuality, recognition of the equality of women with men and increased opportunities for women's participation in all aspects of human endeavour, the pressures of modern life, high mobility and frequent career change. These factors militate against recruiting sufficient numbers of persons for an institution whose leaders and decision-makers are wholly male, which operates from the top downward without integrating perspectives received laterally and from the grassroots, whose record in the area of human sexuality is under scrutiny, and which demands a lifetime and lifestyle commitment.

III. Why must every parish be eucharistic?

Every Christian community has the vocation, in the name of all creation, to offer thanks and praise to God through Christ in the power of the Holy Spirit. It enters into its vocation through anamnesis. As the church's inspired memory, the Spirit makes possible the presence of the assembly to the saving action of God in Christ, which reached its high point in the cross and resurrection. Encouraged by recalling the self-giving of Calvary, the community offers itself according to the pattern of Jesus, its high priest.

Then it invokes God to send the Holy Spirit, that its corporate life might be transfigured and the lives of individual members patterned on that of the beloved Son. En-Spirited, they are invited to enter into personal relationship with the Lord through communion in his body and blood. This covenantal exchange is ordered to deepened personal relationship and commitment, drawing the individual and community into the vibrant life of the three persons.

Actualizing faithful participation in God's action in Christ is the purpose of all sacramental activity. Although in the Catholic traditions every liturgical-sacramental act does not require the presidency of an ordained leader, those in which the church most fully expresses its nature and structure (eucharist, sacramental absolution, ordination) do.

IV. Every eucharistic community needs a priest

It is a sociological given that communities require leadership if they are to maintain their life together.

1. What we do at eucharist

Thanks to baptism, Christian communities are comprised of members configured to Christ and anointed by the Holy Spirit. By virtue of this sacramental configuration and anointing, those who exercise their faith represent Christ in the manifold activities of church and world.

Communities called by Christ, source of their faith, need leaders who represent the presence of the Word-made-flesh, their head, liturgist and mediator. But how can a person act as sacramental sign of Christ, head of the church? This is most easily understood by reference to the eucharistic liturgy, high-point of the community's manifestation of its faith and deepening of its life energized by the trinity.

In a variety of modes—assembly, word, prayer and song, offering, minister, eucharistic bread and wine—Catholic communities experience the Lord actively and concretely present in the celebration. They do what Jesus commanded at the last supper which he shared with his friends. "Do this in remembrance of me": remember me by repeating what I did. Take bread and a cup of wine, praising and giving thanks to God, and offer them, verbally returning to God the gifts of God, to recall that I have poured out my life in self-giving. Offer your lives after my example, in *disponibilité*. Take, eat and drink the bread and cup that I give you as means of the most intimate personal relationship.

Modern historical-critical exegesis has concluded that what Jesus said and did on that night before he died is, in its details, unrecoverable. It cannot be dramatically reproduced or historically re-enacted. What shapes the churches' practice is a primitive and already profoundly rich ecclesiastical exegesis: the witness of faith provided by the communities behind the gospel accounts and 1 Corinthians.

2. Why the president of the eucharistic community is ordained

The eucharist of the church needs to be configured in a manner that unmistakably relates it to Jesus Christ, its servant-leader. But this cannot be achieved through dramatic re-presentation or historical re-enactment.

Following the pope's principle that "every authentic parish is eucharistic" and needs a person deputed by the church to preside at its eucharist, why might not the local bishop authorize laity, including "lay" religious, to preside at the parish eucharist? After all, every baptized member shares in Christ's office of priest, prophet and king; when representing the faith of the church he or she represents the liturgical-prophetic-leadership role of Christ. The question becomes pressing when a parish has a full-time administrator who carries out the variety of leadership functions, preaching and teaching, pastoral care and sacramental preparation that normally fill a priest's job description. Lay presidency is a solution adopted, in situations of need, by some reformed churches.

i) Sacramental signification: leader of a faith community, transparency for Christ, head of the church

When communities gather to share faith and to worship in common, to do deeds of mercy and work for justice and peace, they experience the risen Christ in their midst. When they gather for eucharist in response to the Lord's command to "Do this," they need to signify that it is *really Christ* who invites them to the meal, nourishes them with his word and feeds them with his own body and blood.

We know Christ through faith. In functioning as leader, the ordained priest represents, to the community as well as before others, the faith of the community bound together by discipleship of Jesus. The pastoral leader presides *in nomine ecclesiae* (in the name of the church) when at prayer, the community does what Jesus commanded his followers to do. For instance, the institution narrative expresses the church's faith. Its literary-liturgical form, by interpreting the supper symbolism in light of the Lord's death, discloses the meaning of the community's present action and links it to Jesus' self-offering.

Because the pastoral officer represents at the human, social level (i.e. denotes) the obedient faith of the assembly, that person represents what is ultimately signified (i.e. connotes) the risen Lord, source with the Spirit of that faith. This connotation is what the Roman tradition must refer to when it says that the apostolic officer acts *in persona Christi*.[6] If these two representative functions are not correlated, the priest stands, directly identified with Christ, above and outside the church, and the institution narrative is understood as dramatic re-enactment. Christ, the church's true priest, acts in the midst of and over against the assembly to draw it, through the liturgical action, into his faithful "yes" to God, allowing the members a share in his own response of faith.

Especially when presiding at eucharist or sacramental reconciliation, the priest serves as transparency or symbol of the one who is the assembly's real leader, Jesus Christ. In eucharist this holds, not only for the recitation of the institution narrative, but also throughout the anaphora and the entire liturgy. But there is more. The priest functions as "index" of Jesus Christ and his saving work. There is a real causal relationship to the historical person of Jesus, secured through the ecclesial relationship established by ordination. In the exercise of liturgical office the bishop or priest is not only symbol (transparency) for Christ the head of the church, but also index of apostolicity.[7]

The ordained pastoral officer presides at the community's eucharist and the other sacraments because that person has been established in a concrete, permanent and public relationship to the church through its corporate liturgical prayer and episcopal laying on of hands. In the ordination rite the local church, led by its bishop, has invoked God to send the Holy Spirit so that the minister might be faithful and the ministry fruitful. The church believes that this solemn prayer, made in the name of Jesus, is always heard. The pastoral officer, having received the charism of the Spirit for office, acts as transparency for Christ who sends the Spirit when the church prays.[8]

ii) The permanence ("indelible character") of ordination

Because Jesus was faithful until death in his preaching of the kingdom's nearness, ordination to pastoral office is for life. To exercise church office presumes an ecclesial relationship; in line with the dominant view of theologians until the high scholastic period, the office and its functions may be withdrawn.

It should be apparent from the above analysis why the Catholic traditions have insisted that the president of the eucharist be a personal-sacramental sign of Christ. Lay presiders also represent Christ when they express the faith of the church, but in ways characteristic of the whole *laos*, God's holy people.[9]

V. Back to beginnings

While the renewal of Christian life is never achieved by recreating a "first-century bible-land," return to roots allows us to see how a human institution—in this case the church and its ministry—grows according to the divine plan of salvation, and to discern essential elements of the tradition.[10]

We do not know who presided at the earliest eucharists of the church, which understood itself unitively as *laos*. Probably householders served as liturgical presidents; apostles, prophets and teachers were itinerant ministers certainly called upon for such presidency.[11]

1. Two churches: Antioch and Rome
i) Antioch

Ignatius of Antioch (d. ca. 117), martyr-bishop of that city where followers of the Nazarene were called Christian (Acts 11:26), provides the first instance of a single bishop surrounded by a council of elders and assisted by deacons. The bishop is normatively eucharistic presider. Probably to counter the inroads of proto-gnostics, Ignatius proposes a typology: the bishop is type of God the Father, the deacons are types of Christ and the presbyters represent the council of the apostles.[12] If Ignatius insists that the church should do nothing without the bishop, in turn his deacons and presbyteral council always work in concert with him.

ii) Rome

Initially the church of Rome knew a conciliar style of leadership with a plurality of presbyter-bishops and deacons. The single-bishop type, perhaps imported from Antioch, won the day by the mid-second century. But to speak only of the hierarchy that was to become synonymous with the Roman church is to overlook the crucial role of the house-church in that city as well as almost everywhere in the early Christian mission. Stational liturgies, for which Rome later became famous, unified the city-church while upholding the integrity and memory of these earliest places of assembly. Twenty-five house-churches or *tituli* are documented for Rome; of these nine were held in women's names. Legend places the house of Prisca and Aquila, mentioned five times as friends of Paul, on the Aventine hill. That the householder, male or female, presided over eucharists in these *domus ecclesiae* has gained acceptance among scholars.

Lacunae in the records of church life during the age of the martyrs were supplemented by apocryphal acts and hagiography purporting to make up for missing historical and martyrs' accounts. In the latter legendary accounts, gender equality is present to a degree not found after the Peace of the Church. For example, the Roman *Vita* of

Pudentiana and Praxedis, whose brother is his faithful disciple Timothy, contains none of the teaching on subordination of women and slaves found in the household codes of the canonical scriptures. Implied for women is an ecclesial status equivalent to or in advance of secular society's. The sisters are the spiritual leaders of assemblies that meet in their homes; there at Easter pope Pius (140-155) celebrates baptisms. By the late eighth and early ninth century, popes refurbish or rebuild the sisters' *tituli*. They are depicted as deacons, adding pictorial support for the existence of women deacons at Rome to that of the diaconal ordination rite for women found in pontificals of this period. At some point Praxedis is entitled *presbytera*.

2. The second century

Ordination to the ministries of diaconate, presbyterate and episcopate by laying on of hands and prayer becomes normative in the course of the second century. As institutional structures develop, the egalitarianism of primitive Christianity is submerged. In some churches of the east up to our own day, however, the church is a spiritual family in which patriarchal structures are tempered by love and mutuality.[13]

VI. What of the tradition that only celibate men preside at eucharist?

In the analysis offered in Section IV, ecclesial office is understood by what it does, namely, represent the faith of the church and represent Christ the head of the church, sharing *in the Spirit* of Christ's priesthood. Function and symbolism are correlated. In this theology, aptness for leadership of a Spirit-filled community and the requisite spiritual charisms qualify for ordained pastoral office.

Catholic tradition has excluded persons otherwise apt on the basis of race, marital status or gender. Globalization allows a better understanding of the inequities and injustices of life on planet earth. In generations past, persons were barred from ordination because of race, and for the same reason that ordination of slaves or women was unthinkable: neither could signify headship. Since by definition Catholic Christians are eucharistic, drawn into participation in Jesus' response of faith even to his offering of himself for the world, traditions, however venerable, invite review.

At an early date the city-church of Rome called its ordained ministers to continence. Only with the permanent diaconate established after Vatican Council II have married deacons continued to live with their spouses. The churches of the east have maintained the tradition of the ordination of married men. It is only in this generation that women's full humanity and the practical consequences of baptism for their living the life of faith are being explored. In the early twentieth century scholars established the historical grounds for ordination of women to diaconate. Convincing theological reasons precluding women's ordination to the presbyterate have yet to be advanced.

VII. Reimaging and reconceptualizing the question

What prevents the church from taking the steps necessary to permit communities to be eucharistic? Two chief reasons present themselves: imaging and ecclesiology. I offer for reflection one image at the level of narrative theology and one recent ecclesiological gain.

1. Representation of the Christ who offers communion

Roman Catholics have been accustomed to think of the narrative of institution as the high point of the mass: "Christ becomes present." But the end of every eucharist is realization of Christ's intention to unite himself with his disciples through communion in his body and blood, in order to unite them with God and with one another.

If the end of mass is communion, who facilitates this sharing? Who distributes communion? The integral Christian tradition of east and west understands Christ's role as giving communion with himself ("he offers himself with his own hand").[14] At the level of the liturgical rite the representation of Christ reaches its high point in communion. Women as well as men participate in this ministry as representatives of Christ.

2. Reconceptualizing relations: trinitarian communion ecclesiology

At Vatican II the integral place of the Holy Spirit as bestower of charisms and energizer of the church began to be acknowledged. Consequently all three persons could be kept in view as grounding the church's life. Gradually replacing juridical and Christomonistic communion ecclesiologies (in which the ordained represented, at the official level, God's action in the world), trinitarian communion ecclesiology explains how both lay and ordained Catholics participate in the church's witness, service and worship according to gifts and needs, and how "grassroots" initiatives of the local churches can be honoured.[15] Furthermore, this ecclesiology allows respect for and integration of those differences that enrich the gospel as it is implanted in the spectrum of human cultures.

Conclusion: communion and eucharist

Rather than requiring a single solution as proof of unity, the present crisis urges a reverse move in keeping with communion ecclesiology: maintaining communion while inviting individual churches to provide ordained apostolic officers for their eucharistic "households of faith." In this way the gospel's implantation and inculturation, and the charisms offered by the variety of churches, each of which has gifts to offer, can be acknowledged and received by that venerable church founded by Peter and Paul, and its bishop, guarantor of eucharistic communion.

Notes

1.   1993 statistics from the Canadian Conference of Catholic Bishops show 5342 parishes, quasi-parishes and missions in Canada, of which 1674 are without a pastor, with a gradual decline overall in the number of diocesan priests and a more rapid fall in religious priests. I am indebted to Dr. Brian Joseph for obtaining this data. On factors prompting priestly resignations see Elizabeth Weber and Barry Wheaton, "Atlantic area resignations from the diocesan priesthood after Vatican II," *Studies in Religion* 17/3 (1988), pp. 15-28. For the United States see the brief report, "Priesthood Numbers Slide Said Slowing," *In Trust* (New Year 1993), p. 25.

2.   Based on the report by Jan Kerkhofs, "Priests and Parishes—A Statistical Survey," in *The Right of the Community to a Priest*, eds. Edward Schillebeeckx and Johann-Baptist Metz (*Concilium*, vol. 133, New York: Seabury, 1980), pp. 6-7.

3.   *Ad limina* visit (*Origins* 23/8 [July 15, 1993], 128). "To offer the eucharist for" recalls traditional formulas that accented the priest's role instead of acknowledging the whole assembly as active subject of eucharist.

4.   Above, note 2.

5.   *Origins* 23/8 (July 15, 1993), p. 125.

6.   E. J. Kilmartin, "Apostolic Office: Sacrament of Christ," *Theological Studies* 36(1975), pp. 243-64; *idem*, "Bishop and Presbyter as Representatives of the Church and Christ," in *Women Priests. A Catholic Commentary on the Vatican Declaration*,

eds. L. and A. Swidler (New York: Paulist, 1977), pp. 295-302, esp. p. 297.

7.   The assembly is the indispensable index, which, with its leader, stands in a real relation to the apostolic community. The bishop as leader, teacher and chief liturgist of the diocese is ordained in apostolic succession; as an index pointing to the apostolic office grounded on the apostles, there is a real historical relation.

8.   The charism, or inner content, of office and its relation to the Spirit is developed by E. J. Kilmartin, "Ecclesiastical Office, Power and Spirit," in *Proceedings of the Catholic Theological Society of America* 37 (1982), pp. 98-108.

9.   See Mary M. Schaefer and J. Frank Henderson, *The Catholic Priesthood: A Liturgically Based Theology of Presbyteral Office* (Canadian Studies in Liturgy, no. 4; Ottawa: Canadian Conference of Catholic Bishops, 1990), pp. 57-59.

10.   Raymond E. Brown and John P. Meier, *Antioch and Rome: New Testament Cradles of Catholic Christianity* (New York: Paulist, 1982); R. E. Brown, "New Testament Background for the Concept of Local Church," *Proceedings of the Catholic Theological Society of America* 36 (1981), pp. 1-14. See also Vincent Branick, *The House Church in the Writings of Paul* (Wilmington, DE: Glazier, 1989).

11.   Hervé-Marie Legrand, "The Presidency of the Eucharist According to the Ancient Tradition," *Worship* 53 (1979), pp. 413-38.

12.   The Holy Spirit is still absent from this typology. The *Didascalia apostolorum* (Syria? late third century) will make the deaconess a type of the Holy Spirit.

13.   In 1991 I was privileged, at Varatec Monastery, northern Moldavia, to experience the mutuality which the household model supports. Liturgical and monastic customs of this vibrant Romanian Orthodox monastery (450 nuns, three churches) are in keeping with ancient usages at Rome and other churches of the undivided communion. Sisters live in small groups, five or six to a house.

14.   St. Augustine, *Commentary on the Thirty-third Psalm*, 1.10. This interpretation is one proposed by Prof. Edward J. Kilmartin, S.J.

15.   Schaefer and Henderson, *Catholic Priesthood*, pp. 23-31, based on the detailed analysis of E. J. Kilmartin, *Culture and the Praying Church* (Canadian Studies in Liturgy, no. 5; Ottawa: CCCB, 1990), pp. 33-46. For practical applications of trinitarian communion ecclesiology, see the synod interventions of James M. Hayes (reprinted in *Culture*, pp. 107-111).

Contributors

Romaine Bates (M.A., Education, Boston College), a Sister of Charity of Halifax, is currently in a fifth apostolate as liturgist at Mount Saint Vincent Motherhouse in Halifax, Nova Scotia. She has spent most of her apostolate in education and administration as a teacher and principal. She was director of religious education for the Archdiocese of Halifax for eight years. For seven years she was director of Junior Sisters in her congregation's formation program; for eight years she was provincial superior of the Halifax Vice Province. In her retirement she continues her involvement with the local church as a volunteer on the liturgy committee and catechist for the catechumenate of a local parish.

Normand Bonneau (D. Th., Institut Catholique de Paris, with specialization in New Testament), a presbyter in the community of the Oblates of Mary Immaculate, is professor of New Testament Studies at Saint Paul University, Ottawa, and a lecturer in its Summer Institute in Pastoral Liturgy. He specializes in the letters of Paul, the synoptic gospels and the Sunday lectionary. He is a member of the Catholic Biblical Association and the Society of Biblical Literature.

Patrick Byrne (M.A., Liturgical Studies, University of Notre Dame), is a presbyter of the Diocese of Peterborough. Editor of the *National Bulletin on Liturgy* from 1972 to 1987, and the editorial assistant of the National Liturgical Office from 1971 to 1988, he has also taught at University of Notre Dame in the Summer Liturgical Studies Program and at the Summer Institute in

Pastoral Liturgy at Saint Paul University in Ottawa. He is a founding member of the Canadian Churches' Coordinating Group on Worship and the English Language Liturgical Consultation, has served on the boards of directors of the Canadian Liturgical Society, The Liturgical Conference, and the North American Academy of Liturgy. Currently he serves as associate pastor in St. Mary's Parish, Lindsay, Ontario.

Gerald Emmett Cardinal Carter, D.D. (Ph.D., University for Montreal), spent the first twenty-five years of his priesthood working in various fields of education in his native diocese of Montreal. He was a professor of catechetics for twenty-five years, and authored *The Modern Challenge to Religious Education* (New York: William H. Sadlier, 1963). For the past thirty years he has been a bishop in Ontario, first as bishop of London (1962-1978), and then as archbishop of Toronto (1978-1990). In 1979 Pope John Paul II created him a cardinal. In 1965 he was named to Rome's *Consilium* for liturgy, and was appointed to the newly-formed Congregation for Divine Worship in 1970. He has served as chairman of the Episcopal Commission for Liturgy of the Canadian Conference of Catholic Bishops (CCCB) and of the International Commission on English in the Liturgy. From 1975 to 1977, he was president of the CCCB. In addition to receiving a number of honorary doctorates, he was decorated with the Companion of the Order of Canada in 1983.

Corbin Eddy, (M.Th., Ottawa), a presbyter of the Archdiocese of Ottawa, is director of liturgy for the Archdiocese and pastor of Saint Basil's Church there. He has served regularly as an instructor with the Summer Institute in Pastoral Liturgy of Saint Paul University, Ottawa, and the Summer School of Liturgical Music of the Ontario Liturgical Conference. He has also served as a lecturer in both the Faculty of Theology and the Pastoral Institute at Saint Paul University. He is a frequent contributor to *Celebrate!*, and leads and facilitates conferences and retreats for clergy, religious and lay leaders in the church.

Bernadette Gasslein (S.T.L., Institut Catholique de Paris, with specialization in pastoral catechetics) is liturgical editor for Novalis-Saint Paul University, Ottawa, and editor of *Celebrate!* She has extensive experience in pastoral catechetics and liturgy, and has given many workshops across Canada in these areas. A former project specialist in the youth portfolio of the National Office of Religious Education of the Canadian Conference of Catholic Bishops, she is a member of the Société canadienne de théologie, the Ontario Liturgical Conference and The Liturgical Conference.

Barry Glendinning (Graduate studies in liturgy, Pontifical Liturgical Institute of Saint Anselm, Rome), a presbyter of the Diocese of London, has lectured extensively throughout Canada on liturgical theology and liturgical renewal. He is currently a consultant with the Catholic Office of Religious Education of the Archdiocese of Toronto, and vice-chairperson of the Ontario Liturgical Conference. He is a member of the Board of Directors of the Canadian Liturgical Society and chairperson of the national sacramentary committee. He is a lecturer in liturgical theology at the Summer Institute in Pastoral Liturgy, Saint Paul University, Ottawa.

Regis Halloran (M.A., Liturgical Studies, University of Notre Dame), a presbyter of the Diocese of Antigonish, was the director of the National Liturgical Office from 1980 to 1986, and co-director of the National Liturgical Desk for the Papal Visit, 1983 to 1984. Prior to serving at the national level, he was Director of Religious Education for the Diocese of Antigonish and pastor in several parishes. Currently he serves as chancellor of the Diocese of Antigonish and is the editor of *Guidelines for Pastoral Liturgy*.

Joan Halmo (Ph.D., musicology, with a minor in liturgy, Catholic University of America, Washington), musician, liturgist and musicologist, is adjunct professor in the Department of Music, University of Saskatchewan, Saskatoon. She teaches regularly in the Summer Institute in Pastoral Liturgy at Saint Paul University, Ottawa, and presents workshops and lectures across Canada and the United States. One of her special interests is the paschal cycle. She is author of three books, a number of articles on the paschal cycle, music and liturgy in major liturgical and theological publications. She is a member of the North American Academy of Liturgy, The Liturgical Conference, and the International and American Musicological Societies.

J. Frank Henderson (Ph.D., University of Wisconsin), editor of the *National Bulletin on Liturgy* of the Canadian Conference of Catholic Bishops, is a professor at the University of Alberta (semi-retired), and adjunct faculty at Newman Theological College, Edmonton, St. Stephen's College, Edmonton, and the Summer Institute in Pastoral Liturgy at Saint Paul University, Ottawa. The author of several books and many articles in liturgical publications, he is also a member of the Subcommittee on Translations and Revisions of the International Committee on English in the Liturgy (ICEL) and a former member of ICEL's Advisory Committee. He is a former chair of the National Council for Liturgy, and a former member of the board of directors of The Liturgical Conference.

Raymond J. Lahey (Ph.D., Gregorian University, Rome), bishop of St. George's, on the west coast of Newfoundland, was formerly head of the Religious

Studies department at Memorial University, St. John's, Newfoundland. He is a member of the Pontifical Council for Promoting Christian Unity and a member of the Episcopal Commission for Christian Education of the Canadian Conference of Catholic Bishops. He has chaired their Episcopal Commission for Liturgy and is currently a member of the national sacramentary committee. He is a member of ICEL's original texts committee.

William Marrevee (D.Th., Saint Paul University, Ottawa), presbyter in the community of the Sacred Heart of Jesus, is professor of sacramental theology at Saint Paul University, Ottawa, and director of its Summer Institute in Pastoral Liturgy. He is a member of Societas Liturgica, the Catholic Theological Society of America, the Canadian Theological Society and the North American Academy of Ecumenists. He is also pastor of St. Mark's Church in Aylmer, Quebec.

Mary M. Schaefer (Ph.D., Liturgical Studies, University of Notre Dame), is associate professor of Christian worship and spirituality at the Atlantic School of Theology. She chaired the National Council for Liturgy from 1986 to 1989 and has taught in summer session at University of Notre Dame, Saint John's University and the Summer Institute in Pastoral Liturgy at Saint Paul University, Ottawa. She is the drafter of the Art and Environment Kit to be published by the Canadian Conference of Catholic Bishops, and has contributed articles to a number of scholarly and pastoral publications. She is a member of the North American Academy of Liturgy, the Catholic Theological Society of America, the Canadian Liturgical Society, the Canadian Theological Society, the Canadian Society of Patristic Studies and of the board of the Canadian Corporation for Studies in Religion and the council of Societas Liturgica.

Leonard Sullivan (M.A., liturgical studies, University of Notre Dame), a presbyter of the Archdiocese of Regina, was director of the National Liturgical Office during the crucial post-conciliar years from 1969 to 1979. He chaired the editorial committee of the revised *Lectionary for Sundays and Feast Days*. A writer, editor and pastor, he currently is a member of the national sacramentary committee.

Marilyn Sweet (Master of Divinity, Atlantic School of Theology), the Coordinator of Liturgical Programs for the Archdiocese of Halifax, has extensively studied the ecclesiology of a local church developed in the preaching of James M. Hayes. She has had long-time involvement in the liturgical life of the archdiocese through service on the archdiocesan liturgical commission, and extensive involvement at the parish level in catechetics, catechumenate, liturgy preparation and education, pastoral care and administration. She is a member of the National Council for Liturgy, the national sacramentary committee and a lecturer at the Summer Institute in Pastoral Liturgy at Saint Paul University, Ottawa.

Rembert G. Weakland (M. S. in Music, Major in Piano, Juilliard School of Music, New York.) Archbishop of Milwaukee, Wisconsin, and Benedictine monk, is a noted musician and liturgist. Named a Consultor to the Commission for Implementing the Constitution on the Sacred Liturgy of the Second Vatican Council in 1964, and appointed a member of that Commission in 1968, he was ordained bishop and installed as Milwaukee's ninth archbishop in 1977. He has chaired the *ad hoc* Committee on Catholic Social Teaching and the U.S. Economy, and the Committee for Ecumenical and Inter-Religious Affairs of the National Conference of Catholic Bishops. He is a member of the board of directors of the Wisconsin Catholic Conference and vice-president of the Interfaith Conference of Greater Milwaukee.